EXOTIC FRUIT AND VEGETABLES

Published exclusively for Tesco Stores Ltd,
Delamare Road, Cheshunt, Herts EN8 9SL by
Cathay Books, 59 Grosvenor St, London W1

First published 1985

ISBN 0 86178 302 6

Printed in Hong Kong

ACKNOWLEDGEMENTS

The publishers would like to thank the following companies
for their kindness in providing materials and equipment
used in the photography for this book.

David Mellor, 4 Sloane Square, London SW1;
Elizabeth David, 46 Bourne St, London SW1;
World's End Tiles, British Rail Yard, Silverthorne Road,
London SW8

We would also like to thank the following who
were concerned in the preparation of the book

Series Art Director Pedro Prá-Lopez
Editor Barbara Croxford
Photographer Charlie Stebbings (Laurie Evans page 54; James Jackson page 63)
Stylist Liz Allen Eslor
Food prepared for photography by Jacki Baxter (Michelle Thomson page 54)

CONTENTS

NOTE

Standard spoon measurements are used in all recipes

1 tablespoons (tbls) = one 15 ml spoon
1 teaspoon (tsp) = one 5 ml spoon
All spoon measures are level

All eggs are sizes 3 or 4 (standard) unless otherwise stated.

For all recipes, quantities are given in both
metric and imperial measures. Follow either set
but not a mixture of both, as they are not interchangeable.

We set up our Consumer Advisory Service in response to the many pleas for information and cooking ideas we received from our customers. It is run by our team of qualified home economists who answer queries, offer practical advice on cookery and the home and give talks and demonstrations on new products and equipment.

The resounding success of the service and the continued demand for more and more recipes and information has now prompted us to produce our own special range of Tesco Cookery Books.

Our series starts with 12 books, each one focusing on an area that our customers have shown particular interest in. Each book contains practical background information on the chosen subject and concentrates on a wide selection of carefully tested recipes, each one illustrated in colour.

Exotic Fruit and Vegetables covers an exciting and very popular new area of cookery. We provide essential information on buying and preparation in an illustrated guide and then go on to present a wealth of fascinating recipes. Choose from our ideas for simple starters, colourful main courses and delectable desserts and don't forget the exotic cocktail suggestions at the end of the book.

All the recipes have been carefully tested and offer you the opportunity to introduce a new, healthier way of eating to your family and friends.

I very much hope you will enjoy trying these recipes and becoming acquainted with all the wonderful exotic fruits and vegetables from around the World. Happy Cooking!

Carey Dennis, senior home economist, Tesco Stores Ltd.

INTRODUCTION

It was not so long ago that 'fruit and veg' meant boiled potatoes and green vegetables and maybe the occasional apple or orange. All very well in their place, but a little dull and repetitive when eaten throughout the year. Now, however, the scene has changed and every day brings new and unusual produce to our supermarket shelves.

With this exciting variety (and the ability to buy a few to try which the self-selection system at most large supermarkets encourages) has come a new awareness of nutrition and the part that vegetables and fruit play in the maintenance of a healthy diet. Eating a piece of fruit each day, and vegetables lightly cooked or even raw (in salads for instance), ensures a more than adequate supply of vitamin C plus many other nutrients.

The pages that follow will introduce you to some of the more exotic vegetables and fruit that grace our green-grocery shelves, and reacquaint you with others that are perhaps more familiar. In both cases you will find many ideas and recipes that will whet your appetite to try, taste, and enjoy them.

VEGETABLES

1. ARTICHOKES, GLOBE
Plump, dark green, bulbous buds of a plant of the thistle family. *To prepare and cook:* Cut off the stalk and trim leaf tips. Rinse thoroughly. Cook in boiling salted water for 35-45 minutes. Test if cooked by pulling off an outside leaf, or see if a knife will slice through the base. Pull out the inner purple leaves to reveal the hairy choke, which must be discarded. *To use:* Eat the artichoke by pulling off the leaves with the fingers, starting from the outside. Dip them in melted butter, hollandaise sauce or vinaigrette dressing and eat the fleshy part at the base. Eat the heart with a knife and fork.

2. ARTICHOKES, JERUSALEM
Delicately flavoured, beige-coloured small knobbly root vegetable belonging to the sunflower family. No relation to globe artichoke. *To prepare and cook:* Scrub, peel thinly and plunge into water acidulated with lemon juice. Slice and cook in salted, acidulated water for 25-30 minutes, or dip in batter and deep fry. *To use:* Serve as a vegetable with melted butter or a sauce, use in soups and casseroles.

3. ASPARAGUS
Member of the lily family, grown in many parts of Europe. Long, firm green stalks are best. *To prepare and cook:* Avoid woody stalks. Wash and trim stems; tie in bundles; place upright in an asparagus pan or a pan filled with water to just below the tips. Cook in boiling salted water until tender, about 12 minutes; or steam. *To use:* Serve hot with melted butter, white sauce or hollandaise sauce. Serve cold with French dressing or mayonnaise.

4. AUBERGINES (EGGPLANTS)
Originally from India but now grown all over the world wherever it is warm and sunny. The skin is usually purple-black but some varieties may be green, yellow or pale brown; flesh is white and papery and discolours quickly. Shape also varies from melon to elongated egg. *To prepare:* Wipe, trim ends, then slice, dice or halve. Sprinkle liberally with salt and leave for 30 minutes, to remove the

bitter juices, then rinse and dry. *To use:* Fry floured slices in oil. Bake halves with a savoury stuffing. Use in moussaka and ratatouille.

5. AVOCADOS
Smooth or rough, green or blackish, pear-shaped fruit of a tropical tree with soft buttery flesh and a delicate nutty flavour. Must be ripe before eating, should yield to light pressure on the skin. *To use:* As a starter, slice in half lengthways and brush with lemon juice to prevent discoloration, remove stone. Fill with vinaigrette dressing or prawn cocktail mixture. Make into dips and soup; add to salads.

BAMBOO SHOOTS
Delicately flavoured, ivory-coloured shoots that are cut just as they appear above the ground. If they have any tiny hairs attached to them, remove before eating. *To use:* If using fresh bamboo shoots, strip off leaves and boil gently until tender. Use in salads or in Chinese dishes. Canned bamboo shoots must be rinsed before use.

6. BEANS, GREEN (Kenya or French)
Slender, green long beans which snap when broken. *To prepare and cook:* Wash, top and tail. Steam or cook in boiling salted water for about 10 minutes until tender. Drain. *To use:* Serve hot as a vegetable tossed in butter or in tomato sauce. Serve cold in salads.

7. BEAN SPROUTS
Common ingredient for many Oriental dishes. Produced by placing beans in a little water and allowing them to sprout. The beans most commonly used are soya, mung and curd beans.
Bean sprouts are very nourishing but should be cooked if eaten in quantity.

8. BREADFRUIT
A large tropical fruit with a thick, tough, waxy skin which develops from yellow to brown as it ripens. It is so named because the pale pulpy flesh around the large central core has a mild flavour rather like fresh bread. *To use:* Peel. Bake whole or in slices; fry in slices; boil like marrow; serve instead of potatoes. Make into soup. Most varieties are seedless but if seeds are present, they are edible if roasted or boiled.

BROCCOLI
Green vegetable related to cabbage and cauliflower. Choose close, tightly packed heads with a good, dark green colour. *To prepare and cook:* Remove any wilted leaves, wash and trim. Cook in a small amount of boiling salted water for 10-15 minutes until tender; drain. Or steam. *To use:* Serve as an accompanying vegetable or in soufflés or soups.

9. BROCCOLI, PURPLE
As broccoli above. Wash, trim and cook in boiling salted water in the same way as for green broccoli. (Loses some of its colour during cooking.) *To use:* Serve hot as a vegetable accompaniment.

10. CABBAGE, RED
Deep purple tightly packed head, similar to winter cabbage except for colour. *To prepare:* Remove damaged outer leaves and cut in half. Cut out stalk and shred finely. *To use:* Serve raw and shredded in coleslaw-type salads; pickled; casseroled with apple and onion. Good with pork and bacon. Requires much longer cooking time than green cabbage – 30-40 minutes on top of hob; 2-3 hours to braise in the oven.

CALABRESE
Type of broccoli with a more compact head, may be white, green or purple. Cook as broccoli. *To use:* Serve with hollandaise sauce.

• Pages 7 and 13: A selection of exotic vegetables and fruit; numbers refer to text entries

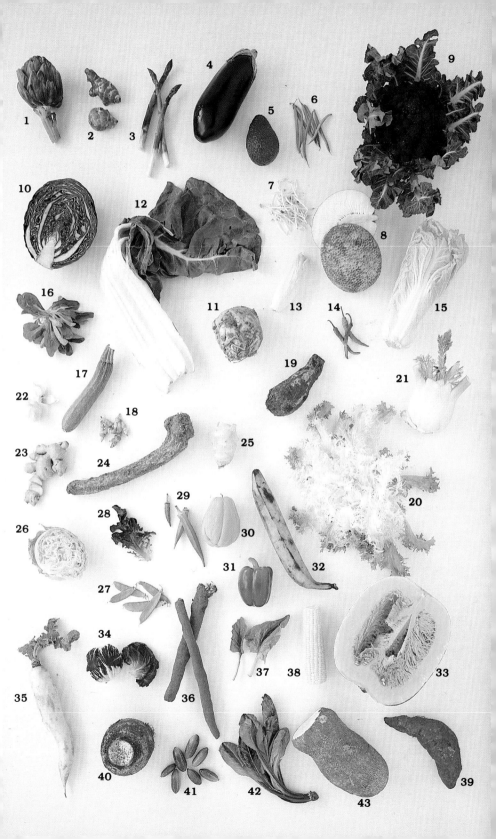

CASSAVA (Manioc, Yuca)
Fleshy tubers originally from Brazil but now grown widely in tropical regions. There are two types, sweet and bitter. *To use:* Bitter is only used after processing. Sweet can be peeled, cubed, boiled or baked whole in the oven.

11. CELERIAC
Root resembling a large, bulbous, rough-skinned turnip in appearance; somewhat similar to celery in taste. *To prepare and cook:* Wash, slice and peel. Dice, cut into very thin strips or grate coarsely. Cook diced celeriac in boiling salted water, with a little lemon juice, for 25-30 minutes. *To use:* Serve hot with white sauce. Or fry strips in butter and serve as a vegetable. Blanch or leave raw, and mix with mayonnaise to serve as a salad. Mash cooked celeriac with potato.

12. CHARD (Sea kale beet)
Originally a southern European plant, chard is related to the beetroot family. It has long, fleshy stalks with dark green spinach-like leaves. Both stalks and leaves are edible. *To prepare and cook:* Leaves – remove from the stalks and cook like spinach. Stalks – scrape to remove any strings then steam or boil whole. Serve with butter or white sauce.

13. CHICORY (Belgian endive)
Choose firm white heads of spear-shaped chicory as green indicates bitterness. *To prepare:* Remove any damaged outer leaves. Scoop out some of the thick base which is bitter. Rinse, do not soak. Cut in half lengthways or separate the leaves. *To use:* Add the leaves, sliced or whole, to salads – good with orange segments, onion rings, watercress and French dressing. Braise in a little water with lemon juice and salt added. Wrap in ham and braise. Serve with cheese or tomato sauce.

14. CHILLIES
Belonging to the capsicum family, chillies grow in tropical and subtropical countries. They are green or red, smaller than peppers, tapered and very hot tasting. *Caution:* Wash hands after handling chillies – they can make your eyes burn and skin tingle. *To prepare:* Trim and chop finely. Remove core and seeds for a milder flavour. *To use:* In chilli con carne, curries and other spicy dishes.

15. CHINESE LEAVES (Chinese cabbage)
Large vegetable with pale, whitish leaves, shaped like a very firm cos lettuce. *To prepare and cook:* Wash, remove base of stalk and cut into quarters. Cook in boiling salted water for 2-3 minutes, then drain. Or shred and stir-fry. *To use:* Serve hot like cabbage, with butter; in stir-fry dishes. Can also be shredded raw and used in salads.

16. CORN SALAD (Lamb's lettuce)
Plant with clusters of small oval lettuce-like leaves grown in Europe and the USA. *To prepare:* Wash and trim. *To use:* Makes a good alternative to lettuce in salads. Cook like spinach.

17. COURGETTES (Zucchini)
A type of miniature marrow, courgettes are best when 10-15 cm (4-6 inches) long and a good deep green colour. *To prepare:* Wash, trim and slice. *To use:* Fry slices in butter or coat in batter and shallow fry. Use in ratatouille. Or halve lengthways and scoop out centre, blanch halves then fill with savoury stuffing mixture and bake.

18. CRONES
Small tuberous vegetable. *To prepare and cook:* Scrub well and cook in boiling salted water. Serve hot with melted butter.

CUSTARD SQUASH
Member of the marrow family, this ribbed round squash tuber is pale creamy beige in colour, and has scalloped edges. *To prepare and cook:* Peel, remove the seeds and slice. Cook in boiling salted water. *To use:* Serve with cheese sauce, or stuffed and baked.

DUDIS
Part of the marrow or squash family, dudis have creamy tasting flesh, and come in several shapes and sizes – they can resemble pumpkin, courgette or marrow. *To prepare and cook:* Top and tail, cut into thick slices, leaving the seeds in, and fry or boil. *To use:* Serve as a vegetable with butter.

19. EDDOES (Malanga)
Root crop of the tropics which comes mainly from the West Indies. They have small central bulbs with many large side tubers, all edible. The flesh is white and the texture is mealy when cooked, with a pleasant nutty flavour. *To prepare and cook:* Treat as potatoes.

20. ENDIVE, CURLY
Crisp, curly green lettuce-like leaves on the outside, yellowish cream inside, both with a slightly bitter taste. *To prepare:* Trim and separate the leaves. Wash well and drain. *To use:* Treat as lettuce. Toss in French dressing; good in winter salads.

21. FENNEL
White bulbous root with a strong aniseed flavour grown in Mediterranean countries. Called Florence fennel to distinguish it from herb of the same name. *To prepare and cook:* Wash well, trim top and slice off the base. Cut in half or quarters. Braise or cook in boiling, salted water for 15-20 minutes, then drain. *To use:* Serve hot with white sauce. Slice raw fennel thinly for salads, or to serve with cheese.

22. GARLIC
A member of the onion family, garlic roots are strong smelling and tasting. The bulb is made up of many individual cloves held together by the white papery skin. Buy in small quantities – a little goes quite a long way. *To prepare:* Chop each skinned clove into 2-3 pieces, sprinkle with salt and crush with a knife. Or use a metal garlic crusher. *To use:* Cautiously! 1-2 cloves is more than enough to flavour most savoury dishes. Use in pasta sauces, curries, and to give a lift to meat stews, salads and sauces.

23. GINGER, ROOT
Knobbly light brown underground stem. India is the world's largest producer. *To prepare:* Peel and shred finely or grate the green-yellow flesh. *To use:* Add to stuffing for fish or to flavour Indian or Chinese dishes. Often used to flavour curries.

24. HORSERADISH
Long, dusty stick-like root of European horseradish plant with a pungent flavour. *To prepare:* Scrub woody skin, peel and grate. *To use:* Mix light white flesh with lightly whipped cream to make horseradish sauce and serve with roast beef or smoked mackerel.

KALE
Member of the cabbage family with curly blue-green leaves that do not form a heart. *To prepare and cook:* Wash thoroughly and shred. Boil or steam and treat as cabbage.

KARELLA (Bitter gourd)
A small, knobbly, green gherkin-like vegetable, bitter in flavour. Grown in tropical countries and much prized in India for its medicinal properties. *To prepare and cook:* Scrape off the knobbles with a sharp knife, top and tail then slice. Put the slices into a bowl, sprinkle with salt and leave for 1 hour. Wash, drain and dry, then shallow fry. *To use:* Cook as an accompaniment to an Indian meal.

25. KOHLRABI
A small vegetable related to cabbage with blue-green leaves, and a swollen bulbous root similar to turnip. Both root and leaves are edible. *To prepare and cook:* Trim off any leaves or roots, scrub well and peel thickly. Leave small globes whole, slice or dice larger ones. Cook in boiling salted water for 30-60 minutes, depending on size, or steam. *To use:* Serve hot with butter. Or sauté slices in butter and serve with chopped parsley.

26. LETTUCE, ICEBERG

A deliciously crisp, compact light green lettuce that keeps well. Grown mainly in California and Israel. *To prepare:* Remove any limp outer leaves, wipe with a clean damp cloth. *To use:* Separate leaves and use in salads.

27. MANGETOUT (Sugar peas)

Flat green pods that are eaten whole with the tiny peas left inside. They have a crisp, juicy fresh flavour. *To prepare and cook:* Top and tail and remove the stringy spine, if any. Cook in a little lightly salted boiling water for 3-5 minutes; or steam. *To use:* Serve as a vegetable with melted butter; use in stir-fry dishes.

28. OAK LEAVES

A member of the lettuce family with dark reddish-brown elegant leaves. *To prepare and use:* As lettuce.

29. OKRA (Ladies' fingers)

Dark green ribbed pods of an Ethiopian hibiscus plant, now grown in many warm countries, especially Kenya. Pods open to reveal sticky flesh and many small edible seeds. *To prepare and cook:* Wash and dry. Remove stem and slice into rounds. Fry briskly with salt and chillies. Or, leave stems on and simmer with tomatoes and garlic, or slit and stuff with spices and cook in a curry sauce. *To use:* Put into casseroles and stews, particularly a Creole gumbo.

PADRUSHKA

Strongly flavoured East European root similar to celeriac. Use sparingly. The green tops also taste of celery and may be used as a flavouring ingredient. *To prepare:* Peel and chop. *To use:* Add to soups, stews and casseroles.

30. PEARS, VEGETABLE
(Chow-Chow or Chayote)

Ribbed, green pear-shaped fruit of a climbing vine of the gourd family, originally from Mexico but now grown in many tropical countries. The flesh is firm and white. *To prepare and cook:* Cut into quarters, peel and remove central stone. Cook in boiling salted water until just tender. *To use:* Serve hot with butter, white or spicy sauce, or cold in salads. Can be stuffed and baked.

31. PEPPERS (Capsicums or Pimentoes)

These mild vegetables may be green, red, yellow, white or purple. Yellow and red peppers are sweeter than the others. *To prepare:* Wash, cut in half lengthways and remove stalk, central core, seeds and pith. *To use:* Slice or dice and use in salads, add to casseroles and stews. Can be stuffed and baked.

32. PLANTAIN

Fruit of the banana family but much bigger and more fibrous. Never eaten raw. *To prepare and cook:* Peel and cook in boiling salted water until tender. *To use:* Serve whole with meat. Or cook, mash, form into balls, steam then serve with butter. Bake in the skins, or slice and fry.

33. PUMPKINS

Large round yellow gourd. The slightly sweet orange flesh is firm and should not be stringy. Often sold in slices by weight. *To prepare and cook:* Wash and cut into bite-sized pieces. Peel and remove pith and seeds. Cook in boiling salted water for about 20 minutes until tender. *To use:* Make into soups or pies, or roast round a joint.

34. RADICCHIO

Small crisp red Italian lettuce with a slightly bitter flavour, similar to chicory. *To prepare:* Wash and shred, chop or use leaves whole. *To use:* Makes a colourful addition to mixed salads.

35. RADISHES, BLACK SPANISH AND WHITE MOOLI

Related to the mustard family, these strong-tasting root vegetables were originally cultivated in China. Black radishes are round and similar in shape to small turnips; white radishes are like long, thin, white parsnips. Eat young before they become woody.

White radishes are rarely eaten raw. *To prepare and cook:* Peel, slice, sprinkle with salt and leave to stand for 30 minutes. Wash and dry. Cook in boiling salted water for about 10 minutes until tender. *To use:* Serve all radishes cooked hot with butter. Serve black or red radish raw in salads.

36. SALSIFY (Oyster plant)
There are two varieties of this vegetable: a long spear-shaped white root, and a black variety (called scorzonera). Both have a delicate taste, rather reminiscent of asparagus. *To prepare and cook:* Scrub well, cut off the top and end of the root. Scrape off the skin, cut into 2.5-5 cm (1-2 inch) pieces and plunge into acidulated water to prevent discoloration. Cook in boiling salted water for about 15 minutes until tender. *To use:* Serve with butter or parsley sauce. Or blanch and add to salad. Make into fritters.

37. SPINACH
There are two types of spinach; the delicate light green summer variety, and the winter or perpetual type which is darker and coarser. *To prepare and cook:* Wash leaves several times in cold water. Put into a pan with no extra water, sprinkle with a little salt and simmer gently for 10 minutes, stirring occasionally. Drain thoroughly. *To use:* Serve with butter. Chop finely, if preferred, or make into a purée. Make into flans, vegetable moulds, soups, salads, soufflés, pancake fillings.

38. SWEETCORN (corn-on-the-cob)
Originating in the USA, corn-on-the-cob is a large stalk to which plump, fresh-looking and pale golden kernels cling. *To prepare and cook:* Strip the greenish husks off the cobs and remove the silky threads. Cook in boiling water to which a little sugar has been added if liked for about 10-15 minutes. Towards the end of the cooking time add salt – not before or the corn toughens. *To use:* Serve as a starter with butter and seasoning. Use corn kernels for soups, fritters and salads.

39. SWEET POTATOES
Edible reddish-brown-skinned tuber originally from South America, but now widely grown in warm climates throughout the world. The flesh is woody and yellowish in colour. *To prepare and cook:* Scrub well. Cook like potatoes for 30-40 minutes, peeling after cooking. Best if boiled and mashed with butter, salt and pepper. Bake or slice and fry. *To use:* Pleasant alternative to potatoes, either mashed, jacket-baked, fried or candied. Make into a soufflé or bake and stuff.

40. TANNIAS
Large tuber of a tropical plant grown mainly in the East Indies. It is the size of a large baking potato with dark brown bark-like skin. Most varieties have white flesh but some are pink or yellow. The slightly nutty flavour is similar to potato. *To use:* As potatoes.

41. TINDOORIS
Like tiny gherkins. *To prepare and cook:* Wash, trim and slice or halve lengthways. Cook with onions, chillies and tomatoes; make into curry with spices or stir-fry.

42. TREVISSE
A member of the lettuce family, with clusters of long slender reddish leaves. *To prepare and use:* As radicchio.

WATER CHESTNUTS
Aquatic bulbs originally from China. Although similar in appearance to chestnuts they are no relation. The delicate white flesh has a fresh, crisp texture. *To prepare and cook:* Wash thoroughly and peel. Boil, stir-fry or roast. *To use:* Add to Chinese dishes.

43. YAMS (Indian potatoes)
Tuber of very large creeper that grows in tropical countries. Yams have brownish-pink rather dusty skin and white flesh. When cooked their flavour resembles ordinary potatoes more closely than sweet potatoes, with which they are often confused. *To prepare, cook and use:* Treat like potatoes.

FRUIT

1. APRICOTS
Small golden summer fruit similar to peach. Grown mainly in warm Mediterranean climates. Choose firm unwrinkled fruit with warm deep colour. *To use*: Eat raw or poach lightly. Use in savoury stuffings for meat, and in mousses, ice creams and preserves.

2. BANANAS
Long, bright yellow (also red and green) tropical fruit, grows in bunches. In yellow varieties, green skin indicates under-ripe, brown over-ripe. Sweet dense flesh which discolours quickly. *To use:* Eat raw; use sliced as an accompaniment to curry; use in cakes and puddings.

3. BILBERRIES
Small blue-black fruit of an English plant similar to the American blueberry. Remove stalks before using. *To use:* Stew; use for pie fillings and to make wine, or sauce for puddings and in muffins and scones.

BOYSENBERRIES
Cross between a blackberry, raspberry and loganberry. The fruit is purple-black with a sweet-sour taste. *To use:* Cook like blackberries or raspberries or eat raw with yoghurt or cream.

4. COCONUTS
The nut of the coconut palm. The hard brown nuts available here consist of a hard fibrous husk containing dense white flesh and milky liquid. Puncture the three small indentations at the top of each nut to remove the liquid, which is not worth drinking. Only the liquid from young green coconuts is drinkable. To open, hit the shell with a cleaver about one-third of the way down from the top to crack, then prise open the shell and cut out the white flesh. *To use:* Eat the white flesh raw or liquidize with milk or water to make thick coconut milk, the basis of many Asian dishes. Use desiccated or creamed coconut in curries, sweets, biscuits, cakes and sponge puddings, pies and ice cream.

5. CRANBERRIES
Small hard red berries from the United States and now becoming increasingly popular and available in this country. They have a waxy coating and very tart flavour. Remove stalks, cook gently until berries burst. *To use:* As sauce accompaniment to savoury dishes, especially Christmas turkey, and in stuffings.

CUSTARD APPLES
There are several varieties which vary in shape and size. The skin of all varieties is green or purplish-green with white flesh and black seeds. When ripe, the flesh is juicy with a sweet-sour taste but some have a sweet custardy flavour. *To use:* Eat raw; add to fruit salads, milk shakes and rich creamy desserts.

6. DATES
Brown, sugar-rich fruit of the date palm, now grown in many warm countries. *To use:* Squeeze the stem end to remove the fresh date from its tough skin. Eat fresh or dried whole; use for sweets and in baking.

7. FEIJOA
A small oval fruit with downy green skin. The flesh is deep yellow, and jelly-like and contains dark edible seeds. *To use:* Peel and halve to eat raw or use sliced in salads.

8. FIGS
Green or purple skin with pale juicy flesh, enclosing a pink heart, figs are grown in Mediterranean countries. Cut the stalks off fresh ones: no need to peel unless preferred. *To use:* Eat raw; or add to fruit salads.

9. GUAVAS
The skin of these round or pear-shaped

fruit from South American or Indian trees varies from yellow to purple and the flesh from pale green to dusty pink. Guavas have a very strong musky smell but an excellent flavour. *To use:* Eat raw or poach lightly.

JAK FRUITS
One of the largest edible fruits. They are usually oval and have thick, hard spiny skin with thick whitish yellow flesh. There are large seeds separately embedded in the edible part of the flesh, which has a delicious banana-pineapple flavour. The fruit turns from green to green/yellow when ripe and has a powerful smell when cut. *To use:* Eat raw. The seeds can be roasted.

10. KIWI FRUITS (Chinese Gooseberries)
Brown furry-skinned, oval vine fruits cultivated mainly in New Zealand. They have sweet green juicy flesh with tiny edible black seeds embedded in the middle. *To use:* Eat raw; peel and slice or chop and add to fresh fruit salads; make into jams and jellies; use sliced to garnish and decorate.

11. KUMQUATS
Small, oval, bright yellow-skinned fruit like tiny oranges, originating in China and Japan, now mainly grown in Brazil. They have a sweet-sour flavour. *To use:* Eat raw, with peel and seeds; make into sauce for duck; use sliced to garnish and decorate.

12. LIMES
Limes, small dark green citrus fruit which have a strong, tart, acidic flavour. Look for a dark shiny tight skin — skin colour lightens with ageing. *To use:* Treat as lemons, although limes have a distinctive flavour of their own.

13. LOQUATS (Japanese Medlar)
Originally an oriental fruit, now grown extensively around the Mediterranean and in the United States. Loquats have a yellow downy skin when ripe and resemble small plums in appearance. The flesh is rich though acid-sweet and

refreshing. *To use:* Eat raw, discarding the stone; poach or preserve in syrup.

LYCHEES
An oriental fruit that grows in bunches like cherries, now also found in Israel and Australia. Lychees have a hard, knobbly, pink-brown shell which needs to be peeled off to reveal the delicate white grape-flavoured flesh inside. *To use:* Eat raw, discarding the stone; use in sweet-and-sour savoury dishes.

14. MANGOES
Oval-shaped stone fruit of a tree originally grown in India and Malaysia, now mainly supplied by Kenya and South America. The ripe flesh is orange-yellow in colour, very juicy, sweet and delicious. Eat when soft and yellow. To prepare for eating you must first cut the flesh away from the stone. *To use:* Eat raw, make into fools and ice creams.

15. MANGOSTEENS
Unusual purplish, reddish-brown fruit the size of an orange with smooth, thick nut-like shells. Cut through the shell round the centre and pull apart to reveal the flesh, which is whitish and juicy, with a delicate flavour similar to lychee. The flesh is divided into segments, some containing a seed. *To use:* Eat raw; add to fruit salad.

16. MELONS
There are many different varieties of melon, a member of the gourd family. The most common are Honeydew, Water, Ogen, Charentais, Galia and Cantaloup. All have juicy flesh which is very refreshing to eat. To test for ripeness, press the stalk end: the skin will give slightly if ripe. *To use:* Cut into wedges, remove the seeds and serve as a starter or dessert; add to salads.

17. NECTARINES
A smooth-skinned cross between a peach and plum. *To use:* Like peaches.

18. PASSION FRUIT (Grenadillas)
Purplish-skinned, wrinkled, round vine fruit originally from Australia and

New Zealand. Juicy flesh is sweet-sharp and contains many small edible black seeds. *To use:* Eat raw, cut in half; make fools and cake fillings; use juice in cocktails and punches.

19. PAW PAWS (Papayas)
These squash-shaped tropical fruit have the texture of avocados and a delicious peachy flavour. They are ripe when the skin turns from green to yellow and the flesh feels slightly soft. *To use:* Eat raw; cut in half, scrape out the black or grey seeds and serve in wedges, sprinkled with lime juice.

20. PEARS, PRICKLY (Cactus fruit)
Pear-shaped fruit which varies in colour from green to pink and is covered in tiny prickles. The flesh is pink-coloured, sweet and has edible seeds. *To use:* Scrub off prickles, peel back skin and eat raw, cut in half or sliced.

21. PERSIMMONS (Italy) or SHARON FRUITS (Israel)
Persimmons look like waxy tomatoes, with orange skin and yellow or orange flesh. When ripe, they are very soft and sweet. When unripe, they tend to be rather bitter. Sharon fruits have edible skins and can be eaten while still firm as they are sweeter and less astringent. *To use:* Halve and eat raw.

PHYSALIS (Cape gooseberries)
Peachy coloured skin encases juicy peach-coloured flesh. The flesh contains tiny edible seeds and the flavour is very delicate and slightly scented. *To use:* Remove the lantern at the top and eat the fruit whole.

22. PINEAPPLES
Succulent and refreshing, pineapples are produced mainly in the Pacific Islands – Hawaii provides almost half the world's supply. The fruit is ripe when a leaf in the centre of the crown can be pulled out easily. *To use:* Eat fresh; slice, peel and remove centre core. Serve with gammon, chicken, ham and cheese and in savoury and fruit salads; make ices, cakes and puddings.

POMEGRANATES
Pomegranates vary in size from an orange to a grapefruit with leathery red to red/brown skin, and filled with small, juicy, sweet red edible seeds. *To use:* Eat raw; chill, cut off the top and eat the flesh with a teaspoon spitting out the seeds. Add to fruit salads. Syrup made from pomegranates (called grenadine) is used in cocktails.

23. POMELOS
Resemble very large pale yellow-green grapefruits with knobbly skin and coarse flesh. *To use:* As grapefruit.

QUINCE
Yellow-orange, tart-flavoured fruit. Flesh is very bitter and rarely eaten raw. *To use:* Make into jellies or jams.

24. RAMBUTANS
Fruit of an Indonesian tree, related to lychees, but covered with soft dark red spines. The outer skin changes from green to red as it ripens and encloses white translucent grape-like flesh and a flat pointed stone. *To use:* Remove leathery skin and central stone, eat raw.

25. STAR FRUIT
Fluted yellow or green, waxy looking fruit, with a delicate sweet-sour flavour. When cut into slices, it forms star shapes. *To use:* Eat skin and flesh together, or peel off the skin if tough.

26. TAMARILLOS (Jambolans or Java plums)
Smooth, glossy, egg-shaped fruit with a light orange, tangy flesh and very dark red, edible seeds. *To use:* Eat raw, halve and scoop out flesh; peel, slice and use in fruit salads; make into jam and chutney; slice and bake and serve as a vegetable.

UGLI FRUIT
A cross between oranges and grapefruit, with a muddy yellowish knobbly skin. *To use:* Eat as orange or halve and eat like grapefruit. No extra sugar is needed.

Stuffed globe artichokes

SERVES 4

4 globe artichokes, stalks removed
3 tbls lemon juice
6 tbls olive oil
4 tbls fresh white breadcrumbs
2 tbls chopped fresh mint
2 garlic cloves, crushed
2 tbls chopped fresh parsley
salt and pepper
150 ml (¼ pint) dry white wine

Cut the tip off each artichoke leaf with kitchen scissors, and use a small spoon to remove the hairy 'choke' in the centre. Plunge the artichokes into a bowl of cold water, with the lemon juice added.

Heat 2 tbls of the oil in a frying pan, add the breadcrumbs and fry over moderate heat for about 3 minutes, stirring, until golden brown. Remove from the heat and mix in half the mint, the garlic and the parsley and season the mixture to taste.

Drain the artichokes and pat them dry. Ease open the leaves and spoon the seasoned breadcrumb mixture into the centre, pressing down firmly.

Place the artichokes upright in a saucepan. Combine the remaining oil and mint with the white wine, season to taste and pour into the pan. Cover and cook gently for 35-40 minutes until the artichokes are tender. Serve hot.

Variation: Use wholemeal instead of white breadcrumbs.

• Stuffed globe artichokes

• Baked avocado with crab

Baked avocado with crab

SERVES 4

2 large ripe avocados
1½ tbls lemon juice
25-50 g (1-2 oz) Gruyère cheese,
  grated
a little cayenne pepper
parsley sprigs, to garnish
For the sauce
25 g (1 oz) butter
25 g (1 oz) plain flour
300 ml (½ pint) milk
¼ tsp cayenne pepper
salt
225 g (8 oz) crabmeat, thawed if
  frozen, flaked

Heat the oven to 180°C, 350°F, Gas Mark 4.

First make the sauce: melt the butter in a saucepan, stir in the flour and cook for 1-2 minutes, stirring. Re-move from the heat and gradually stir in the milk. Bring slowly to the boil and simmer for 2 minutes, stirring continuously, until thickened and smooth. Season with cayenne and salt.

Remove from the heat, then fold in the crabmeat. Set aside.

Halve the avocados, remove the stones and sprinkle the flesh with the lemon juice. Spoon the crab mixture into the avocado cavities and over the top to cover the flesh completely.

Stand the avocado shells upright, each on a base of crumpled foil if neces-sary, in an ovenproof dish. Sprinkle with the grated cheese and a little cayenne pepper. Cook in the oven for 15-20 minutes. Transfer carefully to individual serving bowls. Garnish with parsley sprigs and serve immediately.

Variation: Fry 1 small finely chopped onion and 2 finely chopped celery stalks in the butter for 5 minutes before adding the flour.

Chinese leaves soup

SERVES 4

2 tbls vegetable oil
50 oz (2 oz) butter
1 green pepper, cored, seeded and
    diced
2 onions, chopped
½ head Chinese leaves, shredded
40 g (1½ oz) plain flour
450 ml (¾ pint) chicken stock
salt and pepper
4 tbls single cream

Heat the oil and butter in a large sauce-pan, add the pepper, onions and Chinese leaves and cook gently, stirring from time to time, for 5 minutes. Blend in the flour and cook for 1 minute. Gradually stir in the stock and bring to the boil.

Season to taste with salt, and plenty of freshly ground black pepper. Cover and simmer for 30 minutes, or until the vegetables are tender. Purée the soup in a blender or press through a sieve.

Pour into heated individual soup bowls, swirl a tablespoon of cream over each and serve immediately.

Variations: Chop 2 celery stalks and cook with the pepper, onions and Chinese leaves. Use red or purple peppers to create some colour variation.

Courgette and yoghurt soup

SERVES 4-6

50 g (2 oz) margarine or butter
1 onion, chopped
450 g (1 lb) courgettes, cut into 5 mm
    (¼ inch) slices
900 ml (1½ pints) chicken stock
mint sprig
salt and pepper
150 g (5.29 oz) carton natural
    yoghurt plus 4-6 tbls, to finish

Melt the margarine in a large saucepan, add the onion and courgettes and fry gently for 5 minutes. Add the stock and mint and season to taste. Bring to the boil, then lower the heat, cover and simmer for 20-30 minutes, or until the courgettes are soft.

Reserve a few courgette slices to garnish, then purée the soup in a blender or press through a sieve. Stir in the yoghurt and chill for 3 hours.

Serve in individual chilled soup bowls, garnished with reserved courgette slices and swirls of yoghurt.

Serving idea: Accompany with thin slices of brown bread and butter.

Lentil and celeriac soup

SERVES 4-6

4 rashers streaky bacon, rinded and
    diced
1 medium onion, sliced
100 g (4 oz) celeriac, peeled and
    chopped
100 g (4 oz) lentils
1.2 litres (2 pints) chicken stock
½ tsp dried mixed herbs
salt and pepper

Place the bacon in a large non-stick saucepan and fry gently for 5 minutes until the fat runs. Add the onion and fry gently for 5 minutes until softened.

Add the celeriac and stir well to mix. Add the lentils, stock and herbs and season to taste. Bring to the boil, then lower the heat and simmer for 45-60 minutes until lentils are tender.

Purée the soup in a blender or push through a sieve. Adjust the seasoning to taste. Serve in heated soup bowls.

Serving ideas: Serve with fried bread croûtons or chunks of crusty bread.
Variation: Use padrushka (see glossary) instead of celeriac.

• Lentil and celeriac, Chinese leaves, Courgette and yoghurt soups

Corn with sweet-sour sauce

SERVES 4

*50 g (2 oz) dried apricots, soaked
    overnight*
*1 small yellow or red pepper, cored,
    seeded and diced*
1 small onion, chopped
2 celery stalks, chopped
4 corn-on-the-cobs, trimmed
salt
celery leaves, to garnish
For the sauce
150 ml (¼ pint) malt vinegar
4 tbls demerara sugar
2 tbls tomato ketchup
1 tbls cornflour

Drain and chop the apricots. Place them in a saucepan with the pepper, onion and celery. Cover with cold water, bring to the boil and simmer for about 20 minutes, or until the vegetables are soft. Drain, reserving the cooking liquid, and purée the vegetables in a blender or food processor or press through a sieve.

Meanwhile, cook the corn-on-the-cobs in a large saucepan of boiling water for about 15 minutes or until tender. Add salt only 5 minutes before the end of cooking time. Drain well and keep warm on a heated serving platter.

To make the sauce, put the vinegar, sugar and ketchup into the rinsed-out pan. Blend the cornflour with some of the reserved cooking liquid to make a smooth thin paste. Pour into the vinegar mixture and bring to the boil, stirring, until thickened. Stir in the vegetable purée. Adjust the seasoning to taste, if necessary.

Pour a little of the hot sauce over each corn on the cob and garnish with celery leaves. Serve with corn skewers. Hand the remaining sauce separately in a heated sauce-boat.

Serving idea: Accompany with French bread to mop up the sauce.
Variation: Use a good-quality wine or cider vinegar instead of the malt.

Radicchio with blue cheese

SERVES 4

1 radicchio, shredded
*100 g (4 oz) Danish blue cheese,
    crumbled*
1 tbls thick mayonnaise
salt and pepper

Divide the radicchio among 4 individual serving dishes. Mix the blue cheese with the mayonnaise and season to taste. Spoon the blue cheese mixture on to the radicchio leaves, dividing it equally among the dishes. Serve immediately.

Serving idea: Double the cheese and mayonnaise quantities and serve as a lunchtime dish with crusty rolls.
Variation: Try Stilton, Roquefort or Gorgonzola instead of Danish Blue.

Spinach and courgette pâté

SERVES 6

2 tbls olive oil
1 onion, thinly sliced
350 g (12 oz) courgettes, sliced
350 g (12 oz) spinach, washed
½ tsp freshly grated nutmeg
salt and pepper
227 g (8 oz) carton curd cheese
50 g (2 oz) fresh white breadcrumbs
*2 tsp chopped fresh basil or 1 tsp dried
    basil*
*2 tsp chopped fresh marjoram or 1 tsp
    dried marjoram (optional)*
1 egg, beaten
2 tbls melted butter
courgette slices, blanched, to garnish

Heat the oil in a frying pan, add the onion and courgettes and fry gently for 5 minutes until softened and lightly coloured. Remove from the pan with a slotted spoon and drain well on absorbent paper. Purée in a blender or press through a sieve.

Place the spinach in a saucepan and cook gently without added water, stirring occasionally, for about 10 minutes or until tender. Drain thoroughly and chop finely. Add the nutmeg and season to taste. Place the courgettes in a heavy-based saucepan and set over a gentle heat for 2-3 minutes to dry out. Transfer to a bowl, then beat in the curd cheese, breadcrumbs, basil, marjoram, if using, and salt and pepper to taste. Stir in the beaten egg to bind.

Heat the oven to 160°C, 325°F, Gas Mark 3. Brush the inside of a 450 g (1 lb) loaf tin liberally with melted butter. Line the base with greaseproof paper, then brush with more butter. Spoon half the courgette mixture into the base of the tin, pressing it down firmly and levelling the surface. Spread the spinach in an even layer over the top, then cover with the remaining courgette mixture and press down firmly.

Cover the tin with buttered foil, then place in a roasting tin and pour in boiling water to come halfway up the sides. Cook in the oven for 1¼ hours, or until the mixture feels firm and set when a knife is inserted into the centre.

Remove from the roasting tin and leave to cool completely. Chill in the refrigerator overnight.

Loosen the sides of the pâté from the tin with a round-bladed knife, then carefully turn out on to a serving plate and peel off the greaseproof paper. Serve chilled, cut into thick slices and garnished with the courgette slices.

Serving idea: Serve this pâté with a fresh tomato sauce, accompanied by crisp Melba toast.

● Corn with sweet-sour sauce; Radicchio with blue cheese; Spinach and courgette pâté

Braised pork with artichoke hearts

SERVES 4

75 g (3 oz) butter
450 g (1 lb) pork fillet, cut into 1 cm
* (½ inch) pieces*
1 small onion, thinly sliced
1 garlic clove, crushed
50 g (2 oz) button mushrooms, sliced
1 tsp dried rosemary, crumbled
200 ml (⅓ pint) dry white wine or
* cider*
397 g (14 oz) can artichoke hearts,
* drained and halved*
salt and pepper
1 tsp plain flour
4 tbls double cream
To garnish
strips of lemon zest
chopped fresh parsley

Heat the oven to 160°C, 325°F, Gas Mark 3. Melt 25 g (1 oz) of the butter in a frying pan, add the pork and fry briskly, turning, to brown and seal. Transfer to a flameproof casserole.

Melt half the remaining butter in the pan, add the onion and fry for 2 minutes. Add the garlic and mushrooms, stir well and fry for a further 2 minutes. Transfer to the casserole. Add the rosemary, wine and artichoke hearts to the pan, bring to the boil and season to taste. Pour into the casserole. Cook in the oven for 30 minutes, until tender.

Beat together the flour and the remaining butter. Remove the casserole from the oven, whisk in the paste gradually and bring to the boil on top of the cooker. Simmer for 2-3 minutes, stirring. Stir in the cream, heat through without boiling. Season to taste and garnish with lemon zest and parsley.

● Braised pork with artichoke hearts; Asparagus and ham mousse; Chicory and ham rolls

Asparagus and ham mousse

SERVES 4

225 g (8 oz) asparagus, trimmed
salt
For the sauce
150 ml (¼ pint) milk
25 g (1 oz) margarine or butter
25 g (1 oz) plain flour
2 eggs, separated
100 g (4 oz) full fat soft cheese
pepper
15 g (½ oz) sachet powdered gelatine
2 tbls water
175 g (6 oz) lean cooked ham, finely
  chopped

Tie the asparagus in a neat bundle, place in a saucepan of gently simmering salted water and cook for about 10 minutes, or until tender. Drain the asparagus, reserving the cooking liquid, and allow to cool. Cut 3 of the asparagus spears to about 6 cm (2½ inches) in length from the tip, and reserve to garnish. Purée the remaining asparagus in a blender.

Measure 150 ml (¼ pint) of the reserved cooking liquid and combine with the milk. Melt the margarine in a saucepan, stir in the flour and cook for 1-2 minutes, stirring. Remove from the heat and gradually stir in the milk mixture. Bring slowly to the boil and simmer for 2 minutes, stirring continuously, until thickened and smooth. Beat in the egg yolks one at a time. Cover with cling film and leave the sauce to cool.

Beat the cheese in a bowl until smooth. Stir in the sauce mixture, ¼ tsp salt and pepper to taste, and beat until thoroughly blended.

Sprinkle the gelatine over the water in a small heatproof bowl and leave for a few minutes until spongy. Set over a pan of simmering water and stir until the gelatine has dissolved. Remove from the heat, cool slightly and fold into the sauce mixture. Fold in the chopped ham and reserved asparagus purée.

Whisk the egg whites until they form soft peaks. Using a large metal spoon, fold lightly, but thoroughly, into the ham and asparagus mixture.

Turn the mousse mixture into a deep 1 litre (2 pint) serving dish and allow to set. Garnish the top with the reserved asparagus tips.

Serving idea: This makes a delightful summer lunch, served with a green salad and tomato and onion salad.

Chicory and ham rolls

SERVES 2

3 medium heads chicory, trimmed
  and halved
salt
6 thin slices cooked ham
For the sauce
25 g (1 oz) margarine or butter
25 g (1 oz) plain flour
300 ml (½ pint) milk
2 tsp grated lemon rind
1½ tbls lemon juice
1 tbls chopped fresh parsley
pepper
25 g (1 oz) Cheddar cheese, grated

Place the chicory heads in a saucepan of boiling salted water and cook for about 15 minutes, or until tender. Drain well.

Melt the margarine in a saucepan, stir in the flour and cook for 1-2 minutes, stirring. Remove from the heat and gradually stir in the milk. Add the lemon rind and juice. Bring slowly to the boil and simmer for 2 minutes, stirring continuously, until thickened and smooth. Stir in the parsley and season to taste.

Heat the grill to high. Wrap a ham slice around each chicory head and pack them close together in a 900 ml (1½ pint) flameproof dish. Spoon the sauce over the top and sprinkle with the cheese. Place under the grill for about 10 minutes, or until bubbling and golden brown. Serve hot.

Serving idea: Serve with crusty French bread and butter as a light supper.

• Spaghetti with chilli sauce; Ginger chicken; Sole with fennel sauce

Spaghetti with chilli sauce

SERVES 4

1 tbls vegetable oil
1 onion, chopped
2 garlic cloves
2-3 chillies, seeded and chopped
2.5 cm (1 inch) piece fresh ginger root,
    peeled and chopped
1½ tsp garam masala
1 tsp ground cumin seeds
225 g (8 oz) tomatoes, skinned and
    chopped
150 ml (¼ pint) beef stock
salt
350-450 g (12 oz-1 lb) spaghetti

Heat the oil in a saucepan, add the onion and fry gently, stirring frequently for 5 minutes until softened.

Process the garlic cloves, chillies and ginger in a blender or food processor, to make a smooth paste, or pound them in a pestle with a mortar. Add to the pan with the garam masala and cumin seeds. Stir to mix, then add the tomatoes and stock. Season to taste. Bring to the boil, cover and simmer gently for 15 minutes.

Meanwhile, cook the spaghetti in a saucepan of boiling salted water for 10-12 minutes until tender. Drain and place in a heated serving dish. Pour over the sauce and serve immediately.

Serving ideas: The sauce may be served over pasta shapes, such as spirals, shells or rigatoni, or rice, instead of spaghetti. It would also make a good accompaniment to hamburgers, or to Mexican tortillas or tacos, accompanied by a green salad.

Sole with fennel sauce

SERVES 4

150 ml (¼ pint) dry white wine or
    cider
salt and pepper
2 tsp Barbados sugar
2 heads fennel, trimmed and chopped
8 fillets Dover or lemon sole, about
    750 g (1½ lb), skinned
15 g (½ oz) butter
3 tbls lemon juice
fennel leaves, to garnish
For the sauce
15 g (½ oz) butter
1 tbls plain wholemeal flour
1-2 tbls chopped fresh fennel leaves
142 ml (5 fl oz) carton soured cream
pinch of ground cinnamon

Heat the oven to 180°C, 350°F, Gas
Mark 4. Put the wine in a saucepan and
bring to the boil. Season to taste and
add the sugar, then stir in the fennel.
Cover tightly and simmer the mixture
for 5 minutes.

Place the fish fillets in a buttered
ovenproof serving dish. Pour over the
fennel and its cooking juices and add
the lemon juice. Cover with foil. Cook in
the oven for about 20 minutes, or until
the fish flakes easily when it is tested
with a fork.

Strain the juices into a jug and keep
the fish and fennel hot while making
the sauce.

Melt the butter in a small saucepan,
stir in the flour and cook for 1-2 minutes, stirring. Remove from the heat
and gradually stir in the cooking juices.
Bring slowly to the boil and simmer for
2 minutes, stirring continuously, until
thickened and smooth. Add the fennel
leaves and simmer for a further 2-3
minutes. Stir in the soured cream and
cinnamon. Adjust the seasoning to
taste, adding more sugar if necessary.
Reheat gently, but do not allow to boil.
Pour the sauce over the fish, garnish
with fennel leaves and serve hot.

Serving ideas: Serve with boiled new
potatoes and chilled dry white wine.

Gingered chicken

SERVES 4

4 chicken breasts, about 750 g (1½ lb),
    boned and cut into finger-sized
    pieces
1 tsp sugar
salt and pepper
4 tbls sesame oil
7.5-10 cm (3-4 inch) piece of fresh
    ginger root, peeled and finely sliced
85-120 ml (3-4 fl oz) water
100 g (4 oz) button mushrooms
2 tsp cornflour
2 tbls brandy
1 tsp light soy sauce
fresh coriander leaves, to garnish

Place the chicken on a plate, sprinkle
with the sugar and leave to stand for
20-30 minutes. Season to taste with
salt and pepper.

Heat the oil in a wok or large frying
pan, add the ginger and stir-fry for 2
minutes without browning. Add the
chicken pieces and stir-fry for about 3
minutes. Stir in all but 3 tbls of the
water and the mushrooms. Cover and
cook for a further 5 minutes, or until
the chicken is tender.

Blend the cornflour with the reserved
water to make a smooth paste. Add to
the chicken with the brandy and soy
sauce. Bring to the boil, stirring continuously, until the sauce thickens. Adjust the seasoning to taste. Pile on to a
heated serving dish and garnish with
the coriander leaves.

Serving ideas: Serve with nutty brown
rice or freshly cooked Chinese egg noo-
dles, accompanied by stir-fried mangetout. The Ginger chicken would also
be delicious with sauté potatoes and a
crisp green salad. A light dry white
wine, such as Muscadet, makes an
ideal accompaniment.
Variation: For Paprika chicken, sub-
stitute 100 g (4 oz) chopped shallots for
the fresh ginger root and season the
sauce with 1-2 teaspoons paprika, to
taste. Sprinkle the finished dish with a
little extra paprika.

Beef and courgette Madras

SERVES 2

2 tbls vegetable oil
1 small onion, finely chopped
1 small dessert apple, peeled, cored and chopped
225-275 g (8-10 oz) minced beef
3 tsp mild curry powder
2 tsp plain flour
1 tbls tomato purée
150 ml (¼ pint) hot beef stock
salt
350 g (12 oz) courgettes, peeled and cubed

Heat 1 tbls oil in a pan, add the onion and apple and fry gently for 5 minutes until softened. Add the minced beef and fry for a further 5 minutes, stirring, until the beef is thoroughly browned.

Stir in 2 tsp of the curry powder, then stir in the flour and tomato purée. Cook for a further 5 minutes. Add the stock and season to taste. Bring to the boil, cover, reduce the heat and allow to simmer for 45 minutes, stirring now and then to prevent sticking.

Meanwhile brown the courgette in the remaining oil and curry powder, turning until lightly coloured on all sides. Add to the mince 15 minutes before the end of cooking time and allow to stand for 5 minutes. Serve with boiled rice.

Spinach risotto

SERVES 4-6

450 g (1 lb) spinach, washed
2 tbls olive oil
100 g (4 oz) butter
1 small onion, finely chopped
450 g (1 lb) short-grain Italian rice
1.6 litres (2¾ pints) chicken stock
1 tsp dried oregano
1 garlic clove, crushed
salt and pepper
75 g (3 oz) Parmesan cheese, grated

Cook the spinach in a saucepan without added water for about 10 minutes until tender, stirring occasionally. Drain the spinach very thoroughly and chop finely.

Heat the oil and half the butter in a saucepan, add the onion and fry gently for 3 minutes. Add the rice and stir over a gentle heat for 5 minutes, making sure that the rice is evenly coated but does not colour.

Add a cupful of the stock and cook steadily until it has been absorbed. Add another cup of the stock, the chopped spinach, oregano and garlic. Cook until all the stock has been absorbed. Continue adding the stock in the same way until it has all been absorbed and the rice is tender (about 15 minutes).

Season to taste and stir in remaining butter and all but 1 tbls Parmesan. Pile on to a heated serving dish and sprinkle with the remaining cheese.

Tuna-stuffed peppers

SERVES 4

4 medium mixed peppers (yellow,
  red, green, purple), tops removed,
  cored and seeded
198 g (7 oz) can tuna in oil, drained
  and oil reserved
1 small onion, chopped
12 stuffed olives, sliced
2 tomatoes, skinned, seeded and
  chopped
100 g (4 oz) cooked rice
salt and pepper
340 g (12 oz) can sweetcorn kernels,
  drained, or 450 g (1 lb) frozen
  sweetcorn kernels or peas or mixed
  vegetables, lightly cooked

Heat the oven to 180°C, 350°F, Gas Mark 4. Parboil the peppers and their tops in a saucepan of boiling water for 5 minutes, then drain well.

Heat 1 tbls of the tuna oil in a pan, add the onion and fry gently for about 5 minutes until softened. Add the tuna, olives, tomatoes and rice, stir well to mix and season to taste. Divide the mixture between the peppers. Replace the lids.

Stand the peppers upright in an ovenproof dish and drizzle the remaining tuna oil over the top. Cover with a lid or foil. Cook in the oven for 40-45 minutes, until tender.

Heat the sweetcorn and spoon over a heated serving platter. Arrange the peppers on top and serve hot.

● Spinach risotto; Beef and courgette Madras; Tuna-stuffed peppers

● Chicken salad with sweetcorn

Chicken salad with sweetcorn

SERVES 4

1 tbls plain flour
salt and pepper
4 chicken pieces
1 egg, beaten
50 g (2 oz) fresh white breadcrumbs
50 g (2 oz) butter
1 tbls vegetable oil
450 g (1 lb) frozen sweetcorn kernels
4 small bananas
4 kumquats, sliced, to garnish
For the dressing
284 ml (10 fl oz) carton soured cream
2 tbls white wine vinegar or lemon
  juice
salt and pepper

Season the flour with salt and pepper and use to dust the chicken pieces. Dip the chicken first in the beaten egg, then in the breadcrumbs, pressing on well.

Heat the butter and oil in a large frying pan, add the chicken pieces and fry gently for 15-20 minutes, turning, until browned all over and cooked through. Drain on absorbent paper and allow to cool.

Meanwhile, cook the sweetcorn in a saucepan of boiling salted water according to packet instructions, until tender. Drain and leave to cool.

Peel the bananas and cut in half lengthways. Heat the oil remaining in the pan, add the bananas and fry quickly for about 3 minutes, turning once, until lightly browned. Drain and cool.

Beat the soured cream in a bowl. Stir in the vinegar and season to taste.

Arrange the chicken pieces on a heated platter and surround with the sweetcorn and fried bananas. Garnish with the kumquat slices. Hand the dressing separately.

Aubergine layer

SERVES 4

2 medium aubergines, trimmed and
    sliced
salt and pepper
4 tbls vegetable oil
2 onions, sliced
4 tomatoes, skinned and sliced
50 g (2 oz) walnuts, coarsely chopped
300 ml (½ pint) tomato juice
1 tsp chopped fresh basil or ½ tsp dried
    basil
For the topping
15 g (½ oz) margarine or butter
¼ small onion, finely chopped
50 g (2 oz) fresh wholemeal
    breadcrumbs
1 tbls grated Parmesan cheese
¼ tsp English mustard powder

Place the aubergine slices in a colander
set over a plate, sprinkle with salt and
leave to drain for 30 minutes. Rinse well
under cold running water and pat dry.

Heat the oven to 180°C, 350°F, Gas
Mark 4. Heat 3 tbls of the oil in a large
frying pan, add the aubergines and fry
for about 2 minutes on each side until
lightly coloured. Add the remaining oil
to the pan, add the onions and fry gently for about 5 minutes until softened.

Layer the aubergines, onions, tomatoes and walnuts in a casserole. Season
the tomato juice, add the basil and pour
into the casserole. Cover and cook in
the oven for 45 minutes.

Meanwhile, make the topping. Melt
the margarine in a saucepan, add the
onion and cook for 2-3 minutes. Stir in
the breadcrumbs, cheese and mustard
powder and season to taste. Sprinkle
the mixture over the casserole and
cook, uncovered, for an additional
15 minutes.

• Aubergine layer

Fennel, apple and walnut salad

SERVES 4-6

2 small heads fennel, about 225 g
  (8 oz) each, halved lengthways
4 small dessert apples, quartered,
  cored and thinly sliced
50 g (2 oz) walnuts. coarsely chopped
For the dressing
150 ml (¼ pint) thick mayonnaise
5 tbls fresh orange juice
salt and pepper

Trim the feathery green leaves from the fennel tops and reserve for the garnish. Slice the fennel very finely and place in a large bowl. Add the apples and nuts and stir well to mix.

Put the mayonnaise in a bowl, add the orange juice and beat until smooth and thoroughly blended. Season to taste. Pour the dressing over the salad and toss until all the ingredients are thoroughly coated. Garnish with the reserved fennel leaves.

Serving ideas: Serve as a side salad with cold roast meat or poultry, or with French bread and cheese for a light lunch or supper.
Variations: Celery may be substituted for the fennel, and chopped cashews or hazelnuts for the walnuts.

Celeriac salad

SERVES 4

1 large celeriac, cut into matchstick
  strips
salt
2-3 tbls thick mayonnaise
¼ tsp French mustard
To garnish
chopped fresh parsley
a little paprika

Blanch the celeriac in a saucepan of boiling salted water for 2-3 minutes or until just tender. Drain thoroughly and allow to cool.

Blend the mayonnaise with the mustard in a salad bowl. Add the celeriac and toss well. Sprinkle with the parsley and paprika and serve immediately.

Serving ideas: Serve with cold sliced beef, tongue or ham, or cut cooked chicken or turkey into matchstick strips and combine with the other salad ingredients for a main dish. Serve with wholemeal bread and butter.

Continental mixed salad

SERVES 4-6

½ head endive, trimmed
1 large head chicory, trimmed
1 head radicchio
1 bunch watercress, trimmed
For the dressing
3-4 tbls olive oil
¼ tsp salt
pinch of pepper
pinch of caster sugar
½ tsp French mustard
1 tbls wine vinegar

Separate the endive leaves and place in a salad bowl. Slice the chicory crossways into thin rings and add to the endive. Separate the radicchio leaves and add to the salad bowl. Add the watercress.

Place all the dressing ingredients in a screw-top jar and shake well to blend thoroughly.

Just before serving, pour the dressing over the salad and toss until all the leaves are well coated.

Serving ideas: Serve with hot or cold meats, pasta dishes, quiches or pizzas.
Variations: Corn salad may be substituted for the watercress and crisp Webb's or iceberg lettuce for the curly endive. Diced cucumber, tomato wedges and thinly sliced onion rings all make good additions to this salad. Lemon juice may replace the vinegar in the dressing.

• Left to right: Fennel, apple and walnut salad; Celeriac salad; Continental mixed salad

Stuffed iceberg lettuce

SERVES 4-6

1 iceberg lettuce, trimmed
175 g (6 oz) full fat soft cheese,
* curd cheese or quark*
2 tbls milk
25 g (1 oz) sultanas
25 g (1 oz) walnuts, chopped
1 red pepper, cored, seeded and diced
salt and pepper

Cut off the top of the lettuce and reserve, for the lid. Using a small sharp
knife, scoop out the inside, leaving a
2.5 cm (1 inch) thick case.

Chop the scooped out lettuce very
finely and place in a large bowl.

In a bowl, beat the soft cheese with
the milk until smooth. Stir in the sultanas, walnuts and red pepper. Season to
taste. Add the chopped lettuce and stir
well to mix.

Pile the mixture into the lettuce case
and replace the lid. Chill for 30 minutes
before serving.

Serving ideas: This dish makes a good
party table centre piece.

Serve as a light summer lunch on its
own, with crusty French bread, or with
cold meat or chicken for a more sub-
stantial meal.

Kohlrabi salad

SERVES 4

350 g (12 oz) kohlrabi, grated
1 green pepper, cored, seeded and
* diced*
2 celery stalks, chopped
25 g (1 oz) seedless raisins
4 tbls vegetable oil
2 thick slices white bread, crusts
* removed, cut into 1 cm (½ inch)*
* cubes*
For the dressing
1 tbls malt vinegar
3 tbls vegetable oil
1 tbls crunchy peanut butter
1 tbls tomato ketchup
salt and pepper

Put the kohlrabi, pepper, celery and raisins into a bowl and stir well to mix.

Heat the oil in a frying pan, add the bread cubes and fry for about 5 minutes until crisp. Drain on absorbent paper and set aside. Place all the dressing ingredients in a screw-top jar and shake well to blend thoroughly. Pour the dressing over the salad and toss well to mix.

Just before serving, mix in a few of the croûtons and sprinkle the remainder over the top of the salad.

Serving ideas: Serve as a side salad with cold meats, or as a light vegetarian first course.
Variations: Replace the green pepper with diced cucumber, and the croûtons with salted peanuts.

• Left to right: Mangetout medley; Kohlrabi salad; Stuffed iceberg lettuce

Mangetout medley

SERVES 4

3-4 Chinese dried mushrooms
4 tbls vegetable oil
50 g (2 oz) bamboo shoots, sliced
50 g (2 oz) bean sprouts
1 tbls caster sugar
1 tbls light soy sauce
2 tsp salt
50 g (2 oz) button mushrooms
50 g (2 oz) mangetout peas
50 g (2 oz) broccoli, chopped
1 small carrot, chopped
1 tbls cornflour
2 tbls water
2 tsp sesame seed oil

Soak the dried mushrooms in cold water for about 30-40 minutes. Squeeze dry and discard the stalks.

Heat half the oil in a wok or frying pan, add the soaked mushrooms, bamboo shoots and bean sprouts and stir-fry for 1 minute. Add the sugar, soy sauce and half the salt, stir for a few seconds, then remove with a slotted spoon and set aside on a plate.

Wipe the wok with absorbent paper and heat the remaining oil. Add the remaining vegetables and salt and stir-fry for about 2 minutes. Mix in the dried mushrooms, bamboo shoots and bean sprouts and stir-fry for a few seconds. Blend the cornflour with the water to make a smooth paste and stir into the wok. Add the oil, stir well to mix and pile on to a heated serving dish.

Serving ideas: This is delicious with a Chinese meat or poultry dish, or with plainly grilled pork chops. The salad makes a light main course dish for two if served topped with a freshly made omelette cut into strips.
Variations: Add 50 g (2 oz) extra button mushrooms to the wok or pan with the other vegetables and omit the dried mushrooms. The broccoli may be replaced with cauliflower florets, and the carrot with a small red pepper, cored, seeded and chopped. Spring onions make a good addition.

Okra sauté

SERVES 4

2 tbls vegetable oil
1 onion, chopped
450 g (1 lb) okra, trimmed and
    sliced
1 tsp ground coriander
½ tsp chilli powder
salt
1 tsp garam masala
1 tbls lemon juice

Heat the oil in a frying pan, add the onion and fry gently for 5 minutes until softened. Stir in the okra, coriander, chilli powder and salt to taste. Cover and cook gently for 10-15 minutes until the vegetables are tender.

Sprinkle with the garam masala and lemon juice. Stir well to mix and transfer to a heated serving dish. Serve hot.

Serving idea: Serve with plain boiled rice as an accompaniment to curry.

Candied sweet potatoes

SERVES 4

450 g (1 lb) sweet potatoes
salt
225 g (8 oz) cooking apples, peeled
    and thickly sliced
100 g (4 oz) soft light brown sugar
4 tsp grated orange rind
3 tbls fresh orange juice
1 tsp ground mixed spice
25 g (1 oz) butter
2 tbls medium sherry

Cook the potatoes in a saucepan of boiling salted water for 30 minutes.

Drain and leave until cool enough to handle, then peel off the skins. Cut the flesh into 2.5 cm (1 inch) cubes. Mix with the apple and place in a 1 litre (1¾ pint) ovenproof dish.

Heat the oven to 180°C, 350°F, Gas Mark 4.

Put the sugar, orange rind, orange juice, mixed spice, butter, sherry and

34

salt to taste into a saucepan. Stir well over a low heat until the sugar has dissolved. Pour over the potatoes and apples and toss lightly until they are evenly coated.

Cook, uncovered, in the oven for 1 hour, stirring occasionally, until the potatoes are tender and lightly browned, and the liquid is absorbed.

Sweet 'n' sour salad

SERVES 4

100 g (4 oz) mushrooms, sliced
6 spring onions, chopped
100 g (4 oz) bean sprouts
50 g (2 oz) bamboo shoots, sliced
225 g (8 oz) Chinese leaves, coarsely
  shredded
For the dressing
2 tbls corn oil
1 tbls clear honey
1 tbls soy sauce
2 tbls lemon juice

● **Left to right: Okra sauté; Sweet 'n' sour salad; Candied sweet potatoes**

Make the dressing: combine the oil, honey, soy sauce and lemon juice in a large bowl and mix until well blended.

Add the mushrooms to the dressing and stir until well coated. Stir in the spring onions, bean sprouts and bamboo shoots. Add the Chinese leaves and toss well. Transfer to a glass salad bowl to serve.

Serving ideas: Serve as a side salad with pork chops, spare ribs or cold roast pork.
Variations: Peel, core and chop 1 dessert apple and add to the salad with the bean sprouts. The mushrooms may be replaced by thinly sliced cucumber or blanched courgettes. Watercress sprigs or chopped celery leaves also make a good addition to the salad.

Apricot-stuffed pork chops

SERVES 4

50 g (2 oz) dried apricots
4 pork loin chops, 2.5 cm (1 inch)
thick, trimmed
50 g (2 oz) margarine or butter
1 small celery stalk, finely chopped
25 g (1 oz) flaked almonds
1 tbls chopped fresh parsley
salt and pepper
175 ml (6 fl oz) beef stock
2 tsp cornflour
1 tbls cold water
celery leaves, to garnish

Cover the apricots with boiling water and leave to soak overnight, then drain and chop finely.

Make a slit along the fat edge of each chop and carefully cut a pocket into the meat through to the bone.

Melt half the margarine in a flame-proof casserole, add the celery and almonds and fry gently for about 5 minutes until lightly coloured. Turn into a bowl. Add the apricots and parsley and season to taste. Stir well to mix.

Divide the stuffing into 4 portions and carefully spoon into the pocket of each chop, using a teaspoon. Press the meat back together at the opening to hold the stuffing in place (use a wooden cocktail stick if necessary).

Heat the remaining margarine in the casserole, add the chops and fry to seal and brown on both sides, turning them carefully with a fish slice. Season to

taste and add the stock. Cover and simmer gently for about 1¼ hours, or until tender. Transfer the chops to a heated serving dish and keep warm.

Blend the cornflour with the cold water to make a smooth paste. Add to the sauce in the casserole and stir over low heat until thickened. Adjust the seasoning to taste. Pour the sauce over the chops, garnish with celery leaves and serve immediately.

Serving ideas: Serve with jacket-baked potatoes and buttered carrots, sliced green beans or broccoli.
Variations: Prunes may replace the apricots. Lamb chump chops may be used instead of pork chops.

● Left: Apricot stuffed pork chops;
Right: Plaice with bananas

Plaice with bananas

SERVES 4

3 tbls plain flour
1 tsp mild curry powder
salt and pepper
4 double plaice fillets, about 175 g
* (6 oz) each, skinned*
50 g (2 oz) butter
3 tbls peach chutney, chopped
2 tsp grated orange rind
2 tbls fresh orange juice
2 bananas, peeled
8 parsley sprigs, to garnish

Heat the oven to 110°C, 225°F, Gas Mark ¼. Spread the flour out on a large flat plate, mix in the curry powder and season to taste. Dip the plaice fillets in the seasoned flour to coat thoroughly on both sides.

Melt half the butter in a large frying pan, add the plaice fillets, skinned side up, and fry over a moderate heat for about 2 minutes until golden brown. Turn the fillets over and fry for a further 2 minutes or until cooked through. (Fry the plaice fillets in 2 batches if necessary, adding extra butter as required. Drain on absorbent kitchen paper, transfer to a heated serving dish and keep warm in the oven.

Meanwhile, place the chutney, orange rind and juice in a small saucepan and heat gently, stirring. Cut the bananas into 1 cm (½ inch) slices. Add to the pan and simmer for 1 minute, to heat through.

Spoon a quarter of the peach and banana mixture down the centre of each plaice fillet. Garnish the ends of each fillet with a parsley sprig and serve immediately.

Serving ideas: Serve with mashed potatoes and a green vegetable such as peas or green beans.
Variation: Mango chutney could be used instead of peach.

Spicy meatballs with coconut rice

SERVES 4

750 g (1½ lb) minced lamb
1 onion, grated
2 tbls ground almonds
1 tsp ground turmeric
½ tsp ground ginger
2 egg yolks
salt and pepper
vegetable oil, for frying
2 tbls plain flour
1 tbls tomato purée
600 ml (1 pint) chicken stock
2 tbls mango chutney
4 pieces preserved stem ginger,
    chopped
coriander sprigs or 2 tbls chopped
    fresh coriander, to garnish
For the coconut rice
225 g (8 oz) long-grain rice
50 g (2 oz) desiccated coconut
good pinch of saffron powder
600 ml (1 pint) water

Place the minced lamb in a mixing bowl. Add the onion, ground almonds, turmeric, ginger and egg yolks and stir well to mix. Season to taste. Shape the mixture into small balls about the size of walnuts.

Heat sufficient oil in a large shallow frying pan to cover the base. Add the meatballs and fry over a moderate heat for about 5 minutes, turning from time to time, until lightly browned on all sides. Transfer the meatballs to a plate and set aside.

Stir the flour into the fat remaining in the pan and cook for 1 minute, stirring, over a low heat. Remove from the heat and stir in the tomato purée, stock, chutney and ginger. Bring to the boil, then return the meatballs to the pan. Lower the heat, cover and simmer for 25-30 minutes.

Meanwhile, heat 2 tbls oil in a saucepan, add the rice and fry for 2 minutes, stirring continuously. Add the coconut, saffron and water. Cover and simmer gently for 12-15 minutes or until the rice is just tender. Drain well.

Stir a further 2 tbls oil into the rice and transfer to a heated serving dish. Place the meatballs in the centre and pour over the sauce. Garnish with chopped coriander or sprigs.

Serving idea: Serve with a tomato and onion salad and hand extra mango chutney separately.
Variation: When available, use grated fresh coconut instead of desiccated.

Cranberry pork

SERVES 4

2 tbls vegetable oil
1.5 kg (3½ lb) rolled shoulder of pork
150 ml (¼ pint) water
225 g (8 oz) cranberries
salt and pepper
2 tbls clear honey
1 tsp finely grated orange rind
pinch of ground cloves
pinch of grated nutmeg
watercress sprigs, to garnish
    (optional)

Heat the oven to 180°C, 350°F, Gas Mark 4. Heat the oil in a frying pan, add the pork and fry over a moderate heat for about 5 minutes to seal and brown on all sides.

Put the water into a saucepan, bring to the boil, add the cranberries and cook gently for 5 minutes, stirring once or twice.

Transfer the pork to a casserole and season. Spread with the honey and sprinkle with the orange rind, cloves and nutmeg. Pour the cranberries into the casserole, cover and cook in the oven for 1½ hours, or until the pork is tender and cooked through.

Transfer the pork to a serving dish and carve into slices. Garnish with watercress sprigs, if using. Adjust the seasoning of the cranberry sauce to taste. Spoon around the meat or serve separately in a heated sauce-boat.

Serving ideas: Serve with mashed or jacket-baked potatoes and cauliflower.

● Spicy meatballs with coconut rice; Hawaiian spiced lamb; Cranberry pork

Hawaiian spiced lamb

SERVES 4

3 tbls vegetable oil
2 onions, sliced
750 g (1½ lb) boneless lamb, cut into
    2.5 cm (1-inch) cubes
pinch of ground cinnamon
pinch of ground cloves
2 tbls plain flour
300 ml (½ pint) pineapple juice
juice of 2 limes
300 ml (½ pint) chicken stock
To garnish
lime slices
rosemary sprigs

Heat the oven to 180°C, 350°F, Gas Mark 4. Heat the oil in a flameproof casserole, add the onions and fry gently for 5 minutes until softened. Add the lamb and cook over a moderate heat for 5 minutes, turning once or twice, to seal and brown on all sides.

Stir in the cinnamon, cloves and flour and cook for 1 minute, stirring. Gradually stir in the pineapple and lime juices and the stock. Cover and cook in the oven for 1¼ hours, or until the lamb is tender and cooked through. Garnish with lime slices and rosemary sprigs.

Serving idea: Serve with plain boiled rice and a tossed green salad.

39

Lychee and orange duck

SERVES 6

2 medium ducks, quartered
6 tsp grated orange rind
6 tbls fresh orange juice
283 g (10 oz) can lychees, drained,
*   syrup reserved or 450 g (1 lb) fresh*
*   lychees, peeled and stoned*
salt and pepper
50 g (2 oz) butter, diced
1 tbls cornflour
300 ml (½ pint) chicken stock
2 tbls coarse-cut orange marmalade
watercress sprigs, to garnish

Prick the duck skin all over with a fork. Arrange the duck pieces cut side down, in a shallow dish and pour over the orange rind and juice and the lychee syrup and season to taste. Cover with cling film and chill in the refrigerator for 6-8 hours or overnight.

Heat the oven to 200°C, 400°F, Gas Mark 6. Lift the ducks from the marinade, reserving the marinade, and place cut side down on a trivet in a roasting tin. Dot with the butter and roast in the oven for 45 minutes, basting frequently, until tender and cooked through.

Meanwhile, blend the cornflour smoothly with the chicken stock in a bowl. Add the marinade and marmalade, then pour into a saucepan.

When the ducks are cooked, transfer to a heated serving dish and keep warm. Drain the fat from the roasting tin. Stir the sauce ingredients in the saucepan over low heat until thickened, then add the juices from the roasting tin.

Add the lychees to the sauce and heat through gently. Spoon the sauce over the duck, garnish with watercress sprigs and serve immediately.

Serving idea: Serve with new potatoes cooked in their skins and a tossed green salad.
Variation: If using fresh lychees, add a little extra orange juice.

Cold smoked pork with mango mayonnaise

SERVES 4

3 tbls mango chutney
6 tbls thick mayonnaise
salt and pepper
1 small iceberg lettuce, shredded
½ cucumber, sliced
350 g (12 oz) cold smoked pork, sliced
fresh or canned, drained mango
*   slices, to garnish*

Stir the chutney into the mayonnaise and season to taste. Place the lettuce and cucumber in a salad bowl.

Arrange the cold pork on a serving platter and garnish with mango slices. Spoon a little of the mango mayonnaise into the centre and hand round the remainder separately in a bowl.

Mexican ceviche

SERVES 4

• Left: Lychee and orange duck; Centre:
Mexican ceviche; Right: Cold smoked
pork with mango mayonnaise

8 fillets lemon sole or plaice, about
 750g (1 ½ lb), skinned
juice of 5 limes
4 tbls olive oil
1 tbls chopped fresh coriander or
 parsley
salt and pepper
1 large tomato, skinned and chopped
4 spring onions, chopped
1 red chilli, seeded and chopped
coriander or parsley sprigs, to garnish

Cut the fish fillets diagonally into 7 mm
(⅓ inch) strips and place in a bowl.
Pour over the lime juice. Cover the bowl
and chill in the refrigerator for 24
hours, spooning the juices over the fish
from time to time.

Drain off and discard the juice. In a
bowl, toss the fish strips in the oil and
coriander and season to taste. Add the
tomato, spring onions and chilli and
stir well to mix, adding a little extra oil,
if necessary. Adjust the seasoning to
taste if necessary.

Serve in scallop shells or ramekin
dishes, garnished with coriander or
parsley sprigs.

Serving ideas: Serve as a no-cook
starter with hot garlic bread, or with a
rice salad for a no-cook summer lunch
or supper dish.

Devilled gammon with nectarines

SERVES 4

4 gammon steaks, about 100-175 g
    (4-6 oz) each, rind removed
25 g (1 oz) butter, melted
100 g (4 oz) mushrooms
1 tbls French mustard
2 tbls demerara sugar
4 fresh nectarines, skinned, halved
    and stoned
watercress sprigs, to garnish

Snip the fat at 1 cm (½ inch) intervals around the gammon steaks to prevent them curling under the grill. Heat the grill to moderate.

Brush one side of the steaks with melted butter and arrange on the grill rack.

Brush the mushrooms all over with melted butter and place in the grill pan, under the rack.

Grill for 5 minutes, then turn the steaks. Brush with more butter, spread lightly with mustard and sprinkle with 1 tbls of the sugar. Grill for a further 3 minutes.

Arrange a nectarine half on each steak, brush with the remaining butter and sprinkle with the remaining sugar. Grill for a further 2 minutes to lightly glaze the nectarines, increasing the heat if necessary.

Transfer the gammon steaks to a heated serving dish, garnish with the cooked mushrooms and watercress sprigs and serve immediately.

Serving ideas: Serve with sauté or creamed potatoes and sliced runner beans or peas.
Variation: Fresh or canned, drained pineapple rings could be used instead of nectarines.

● Left to right: Pineapple chicken;
Devilled gammon with nectarines;
Pomegranate chicken

Pineapple chicken

SERVES 4

1.75 kg (3½ lb) oven-ready chicken
50 g (2 oz) butter
2 shallots, chopped
salt and pepper
For the stuffing
½ small pineapple, peeled, cored and
    chopped
75 g (3 oz) cooked brown rice
25 g (1 oz) chopped walnuts
25 g (1 oz) melted butter
salt and pepper
To garnish
large slice pineapple, peeled, cored
    and cut into triangles
watercress sprigs

Heat the oven to 200°C, 400°F, Gas Mark 6. Melt the butter in a roasting tin, add the shallots and cook gently for 5 minutes until softened. Add the chicken and fry for about 10 minutes to seal and brown lightly on all sides.

Combine the ingredients for the

stuffing, season, and bind well together. Loosely fill the body of the chicken with the mixture. Roast in the oven for 1¼ hours, or until tender.

Transfer the chicken to a heated serving dish and keep hot. Add the pineapple triangles to the roasting tin and fry gently, turning once, until the pineapple is heated through, then use to garnish along with the watercress.

Pomegranate chicken

SERVES 4

25 g (1 oz) butter
3 onions, chopped
175-225 g (6-8 oz) walnuts, chopped
900 ml (1½ pints) water
salt and pepper
10 tbls pomegranate syrup or juice
4 tbls sugar
4 chicken pieces
To garnish
walnut halves
pomegranate slices

Melt the butter in a flameproof casserole, add the onions and fry gently for 5 minutes until softened. Stir in the walnuts and cook for a further 5 minutes. Pour in the water and season to taste.

Bring to the boil, stir in the pomegranate juice and sugar and simmer for 30 minutes. Stir frequently to prevent the walnuts sticking to the bottom of the pan.

Add the chicken, cover and simmer gently for about 1 hour, or until the chicken is tender and cooked through.

Transfer the chicken to a heated serving dish, pour over the sauce and garnish with walnut halves and pomegranate slices. Serve the Pomegranate chicken immediately.

Serving ideas: Serve with rice, with toasted almonds and sultanas, and a salad. Serve a chilled rosé wine with the Pomegranate chicken.
Variation: The chicken may be replaced by duck, which is traditionally used in this dish in Iran, from where it originates.

Apricot and brandy trifle

SERVES 4-6

150 ml (¼ pint) sweet white wine
50 g (2 oz) caster sugar
450 g (1 lb) ripe apricots, halved and
  stoned
85 ml (3 fl oz) brandy
225 g (8 oz) ratafia biscuits
142 ml (5 fl oz) carton double or
  whipping cream
For the custard
3 eggs, beaten
2 tbls sugar
1 tbls cornflour
600 ml (1 pint) milk

To make the custard, place the eggs and sugar in the top part of a double saucepan, or in a flameproof bowl set over a saucepan of simmering water, and whisk until pale and creamy. Blend the cornflour with a little of the milk to make a smooth paste and whisk into the egg mixture. Whisk in the milk and cook for about 10 minutes, stirring continuously, until thickened and smooth. Pour the custard into a bowl and whisk gently. Allow to cool.

Place the wine and sugar in a saucepan and bring slowly to the boil. Stir until the sugar has dissolved, then add the apricot halves and cook gently for about 5 minutes, or until softened. Remove from the heat and allow to cool.

Place the apricots in a glass serving bowl and pour over the syrup and brandy. Reserve 6 of the ratafia biscuits for decoration, crush the remainder and sprinkle over the apricots. Spoon the cooled custard over the biscuits and chill in the refrigerator for 3 hours.

Just before serving, whip the cream and pipe or spoon over the trifle. Decorate with the reserved ratafia biscuits.

Avocado and banana mousse

SERVES 3-4

1 large banana, peeled
1 ripe avocado, halved, stoned and
  peeled
2 tbls lemon juice
4 tsp caster sugar
1 egg white
25 g (1 oz) plain chocolate, grated

Roughly chop the banana and avocado flesh. Add the lemon juice and sugar. Purée the mixture in a blender or press through a sieve.

Whisk the egg white stiffly and fold it into the purée. Divide the mixture between 3-4 individual dessert dishes. Decorate each one with grated chocolate. Chill in the refrigerator for at least 2 hours before serving.

Serving idea: Serve with sponge fingers.
Variation: Decorate with banana slices dipped in fresh lemon juice to prevent discoloration.

Banana and ginger pancakes

SERVES 6

For the batter
100 g (4 oz) plain flour
1 egg, beaten
300 ml (½ pint) milk
vegetable oil, for frying
For the filling
6 firm bananas, peeled
1 tbls lemon juice
50 g (2 oz) butter
50 g (2 oz) caster sugar
2 tsp ground ginger

To make the batter, sift the flour into a mixing bowl and make a well in the centre. Add the egg and half the milk, drawing the flour into the milk with a wooden spoon; beat well to make a smooth batter. Stir in the remaining milk and beat well again.

Lightly oil a 20 cm (8 inch) frying pan, heat and pour in an eighth of the batter. Tilt pan so that batter runs evenly over the base. Cook for 1-2 minutes until the batter is set and bubbles form on the surface. Using a fish slice, carefully turn the pancake and cook until the underside is golden. Fry the remaining pancakes until all the batter is used up, stacking them on a plate with greaseproof paper between each one.

Cut the bananas in half lengthways then crossways into quarters. Sprinkle them with the lemon juice. Melt half the butter in a frying pan, add the bananas and fry gently, turning, for about 5 minutes until just beginning to brown. Using a slotted spoon, remove the bananas from the pan and toss in the sugar combined with the ginger.

Heat the oven to 190°C, 375°F, Gas Mark 5. Place a portion of the banana filling on the centre of each pancake, dividing it equally among them. Fold over the sides of each pancake and arrange in a buttered ovenproof dish. Melt the remaining butter and drizzle it over the pancakes.

Cover and bake in the oven for 20 minutes until heated through.

Serving idea: Serve sprinkled with caster sugar and cream.

Variations: Apple and cinnamon pancakes: fill with 450 g (1 lb) sliced cooking apples, fried in butter, then sweetened to taste with sugar and ground cinnamon.

Apricot and almond pancakes: fill with 425 g (15 oz) can apricots, drained and chopped with 25 g (1 oz) toasted, chopped almonds.

Orange pancakes: flavour the batter with 3 tsp grated orange rind and pour 4 tbls orange juice over the pancakes.

● Avocado and banana mousse; Apricot and brandy trifle; Banana and ginger pancakes

Coconut and cherry cake

MAKES ONE 20 cm (8 inch) round cake

300 g (12 oz) self-raising flour
pinch of salt
175 g (6 oz) hard margarine, diced
225 g (8 oz) glacé cherries, washed,
dried and quartered
50 g (2 oz) desiccated coconut
175 g (6 oz) caster sugar
2 large eggs, lightly beaten
150 ml (¼ pint) milk

Well grease a 20 cm (8 inch) round cake tin and line the base with greased greaseproof paper. Heat the oven to 180°C, 350°F, Gas Mark 4.

Sift the flour with the salt into a mixing bowl. Add the margarine and rub it in with the fingertips until the mixture resembles fine breadcrumbs. Toss the cherries in the coconut and stir into the mixture with the sugar. Stir in the eggs with most of the milk, beat well and add a little extra milk to give a soft dropping consistency. Turn the mixture into the prepared tin and level the top.

Bake the cake in the oven for 1½ hours, or until well risen and golden brown, and a fine skewer inserted into the centre comes out clean. Remove from the oven and leave in the tin for 5 minutes, then turn on to a wire rack and leave to cool completely.

Bilberry muffins

MAKES 18-20

150 g (5 oz) butter, softened
450 g (1 lb) bilberries (or blueberries),
hulled if fresh
225 g (8 oz) plain or wholemeal flour
2 tsp baking powder
½ tsp salt
50 g (2 oz) light brown sugar
2 eggs
75 ml (3 fl oz) milk

Heat the oven to 190°C, 375°F, Gas Mark 5. Generously grease 18-20 muffin, patty or bun tins with softened butter and set aside.

Purée about a third of the berries and set aside. Toss the remainder in 25 g (1 oz) of the flour. Mix the remaining flour, baking powder and salt together. Beat the remaining butter with the sugar until light and fluffy. Gradually beat in the eggs then about half the flour mixture, beating until incorporated. Add half the milk, then the remaining flour and milk until the mixture forms a smooth batter. Fold in the puréed berries then the whole ones.

Divide the batter among the prepared tins, filling each one about two-thirds full. Bake in the oven for 15-20 minutes or until the muffins are golden brown. Transfer to a wire rack to cool.

Serving ideas: Serve warm, for breakfast or as an after-school snack. Split and toast and serve buttered.

Cranberry mincemeat jalousie

SERVES 4-6

175 g (6 oz) fresh or frozen cranberries
1 tbls water
25 g (1 oz) sugar
225 g (8 oz) mincemeat
50 g (2 oz) shelled walnuts, chopped
350 g (12 oz) frozen puff pastry,
thawed
1 egg, beaten
3 tbls golden syrup or clear honey

Heat the oven to 220°C, 425°F, Gas Mark 7. Place the cranberries, water and sugar in a saucepan and simmer gently for 5-10 minutes, or until they start to pop. Remove from the heat and allow to cool slightly, then stir in the mincemeat and walnuts.

Roll out the pastry on a lightly floured surface to a 46 × 18 cm (18 × 7 inch) rectangle. Cut crossways into two 23 × 18 cm (9 × 7 inch) rectangles.

Place one pastry rectangle on a dampened baking sheet. Spoon over the cranberry and mincemeat mixture, to

• Bilberry muffins; Coconut and cherry cake; Cranberry mincemeat jalousie

within 2 cm (¾ inch) of the edges. Moisten the pastry edges.

Fold the other pastry rectangle in half lengthways and, using a floured knife, make crossways cuts 1 cm (½ inch) apart to within 2 cm (¾ inch) of the edge. Open out the pastry and position over the first piece. Press the edges together firmly to seal, knock up and flute. Brush the pastry all over with beaten egg to glaze.

Bake in the oven for 20-25 minutes, or until the pastry is crisp and golden. Remove from the oven and brush immediately with the golden syrup. Transfer to a wire tray to cool.

Variation: Omit the cranberries, sugar and walnuts. Instead simmer 350 g (12 oz) peeled, cored and chopped cooking apples with the water for about 5 minutes until just tender. Cool and stir in the mincemeat and use as a filling for the jalousie.

Date and walnut fingers

MAKES 8

For the pastry
100 g (4 oz) plain flour
pinch of salt
25 g (1 oz) margarine, diced
25 g (1 oz) lard, diced
1 tbls water
For the filling
225 g (8 oz) caster sugar
100 g (4 oz) ground almonds
150 g (5 oz) stoned dates, chopped
50 g (2 oz) shelled walnuts, chopped
2 eggs, beaten
For the icing
50 g (2 oz) icing sugar, sifted
1 tbls warm water
walnut halves, to finish

Heat the oven to 200°C, 400°F, Gas Mark 6. To make the pastry, sift the flour with the salt into a mixing bowl. Add the margarine and lard and rub in with the fingertips until the mixture resembles fine breadcrumbs. Add the water and mix with a round-bladed knife, to form a fairly firm dough.

Grease a shallow rectangular tin about 20 × 10 cm (8 × 4 inches). Roll out the pastry thinly on a lightly floured board or work surface and use to line the base and sides of tin. Trim edges.

Combine the sugar, almonds, dates and walnuts in a bowl. Add the beaten eggs and stir well to mix. Spoon the mixture into the prepared tin and spread out evenly.

Bake in the oven for 20 minutes, then reduce the oven temperature to 190°C, 375°F, Gas Mark 5 and bake for a further 20 minutes. Remove from the oven and allow to cool in the tin, then turn on to a wire rack. To make the icing, blend the icing sugar with the water. Spread over the top of the cake and leave to set, then cut into fingers. Decorate with walnut halves.

Serving ideas: Serve for tea or as part of a picnic.
Variation: Use chopped dried figs instead of dates.

Carnival figs

SERVES 4

8 fresh figs
142 ml (5 fl oz) carton soured cream
4 tbls crème de cacao
grated chocolate or fig slices, to
  decorate

Place the figs in a heatproof bowl, pour over boiling water to cover and leave for 1 minute. Drain thoroughly and peel off the skins. Cut each fig into quarters.

Combine the soured cream and crème de cacao in a serving bowl. Fold in the fig pieces and decorate with grated chocolate or sliced fig. Chill for at least 1 hour before serving.

Serving idea: Accompany with crisp biscuits such as brandy snaps.
Variation: Use orange curaçao instead of crème de cacao – and decorate with grated orange rind.

● Left: Carnival figs;
Centre: Kiwi meringues;
Right: Date and walnut fingers

Kiwi meringues

SERVES 4

142 ml (5 fl oz) carton double cream
1 egg white
2 tbls icing sugar, sifted
2 kiwi fruit, peeled and chopped
1 kiwi fruit, peeled and sliced, to decorate
For the meringue baskets
4 egg whites
pinch of salt
240-275 g (8½-10 oz) icing sugar, sifted

To make the baskets, line a large baking sheet with non-stick silicone paper. Place the egg whites in a bowl and whisk until foaming but not quite stiff. Mix in the salt. Whisk in the icing sugar, 1 tbls at a time, until the mixture is very stiff and glossy.

Heat the oven to 130°C, 250°F, Gas Mark ½. Place the meringue mixture in a piping bag fitted with a plain nozzle. Pipe 4 × 7.5 cm (3 inch) circles on to the prepared baking sheet. Change to a rosette nozzle and pipe rosettes round the edges of each circle to make a basket. Bake in the oven for about 50 minutes, until the baskets are dried out.

Remove from the oven and carefully peel off the lining paper, then leave the meringue baskets to cool completely before making the filling.

Whip the cream and egg white together until light and thick. Using a metal spoon, fold in the icing sugar. Stir in the chopped kiwi fruit.

Arrange the meringue baskets on a serving dish, spoon the cream and kiwi mixture into the baskets and decorate with the kiwi slices.

Serving ideas: The kiwi meringues make a perfect special occasion dessert. As they are easy to eat with a fork, they are ideal to serve as part of a buffet supper. Or they may be served for an elegant afternoon tea.

Variations: To make a really colourful dessert for a dinner party, fill the meringue baskets with different exotic fruits, such as paw paw, mango and nectarines. Or fill with mango ice cream and decorate with slices of the fruit.

Grapefruit and melon jelly

SERVES 6

600 ml (1 pint) unsweetened grapefruit juice
3 × 15 g (½oz) sachets powdered gelatine
1 honeydew melon, about 1.25 kg (2½-2¾lb), peeled, seeded and coarsely chopped
To decorate
whipped cream
slices of stem ginger (optional)

Place 6 tbls of the grapefruit juice in a heatproof bowl, sprinkle over the gelatine and leave until spongy. Put the bowl in a saucepan of hot water and stir until the gelatine has dissolved. Stir in the remaining grapefruit juice. Chill in the refrigerator until the mixture is the consistency of unbeaten egg white.

Stir the melon flesh into the jelly. Spoon the mixture into a wetted 1.2 litre (2 pint) jelly mould. Chill the grapefruit and melon jelly in the refrigerator for 3-4 hours or until set firm.

To serve, dip the mould for a few seconds in boiling water, place an inverted serving plate over the mould and invert to unmould. Decorate the jelly with swirls of whipped cream and slices of stem ginger, if liked.

Serving idea: For a very attractive finish make a little extra jelly and leave to set in a saucer. When set, chop and use to decorate base of unmoulded jelly. *Variations:* Use any fruit juice such as orange, pineapple, apple or grape with fresh fruit added to complement the flavour of the jelly.

Tangy lime mousse

SERVES 8

25 g (1 oz) cornflour
450 ml (¾ pint) milk
100 g (4 oz) caster sugar
3 eggs, separated
8 tsp finely grated lime rind
4 tbls fresh lime juice
15 g (½oz) sachet powdered gelatine
few drops of green food colouring
To decorate
lime twists
whipped cream

In a bowl, blend the cornflour with a little of the milk to make a smooth paste. Beat in the sugar and egg yolks.

Heat the remaining milk to just below boiling point and stir into the mix-

● Left: Grapefruit and melon jelly;
Centre: Tangy lime mousse;
Right: Lychee ice cream

ture. Return the pan to the heat and cook for about 2 minutes, stirring, until the mixture is thickened. Remove from the heat and stir in the lime rind.

Place the lime juice in a small heatproof bowl, sprinkle over the gelatine and leave for a few minutes until spongy. Set the bowl in a saucepan of hot water and stir until the gelatine has dissolved. Stir into the custard. Add 1-2 drops of green food colouring.

Whisk the egg whites stiffly, then fold into the mixture, using a large metal spoon. Spoon into 4 individual serving dishes and chill in the refrigerator for at least 2 hours until firm.

Decorate with lime twists and whipped cream.

Variation: Use lemon rind, juice and twists instead of lime.

Lychee ice cream

SERVES 4-6

410g (14½oz) can evaporated milk,
  chilled in the refrigerator overnight
100g (4oz) icing sugar, sifted
560g (1¼lb) can lychees, drained
  and chopped

In a bowl whisk the chilled evaporated milk until thick and frothy, then whisk in the icing sugar. Lightly fold in the chopped lychees.

Pour into a rigid freezerproof container and freeze for 4 hours, beating the mixture 3 times, at hourly intervals.

Serving idea: Serve scoops of ice cream with canned or fresh lychees and sponge fingers or crisp sweet biscuits.

51

Mango ice cream

SERVES 4

*350 g (12 oz) mango flesh, fresh or
canned and drained
2 eggs, separated
50 g (2 oz) caster sugar
142 ml (5 fl oz) carton double cream
4 tbls lemon juice*

Purée the mango flesh in a blender or
food processor.

Whisk the egg whites until they form
soft peaks. Gradually whisk in the
sugar until stiff and glossy.

Whip the cream until thick. Lightly
beat in the egg yolks. Carefully fold the
whisked egg whites into the cream and
yolk mixture until well blended, then
stir in the mango purée and lemon
juice.

Turn the mixture into a rigid freezerproof container and freeze for at least 6
hours. An hour before serving, place
the ice cream in the refrigerator to
soften slightly.

Melon and ginger ice cream

SERVES 4-6

*750 g (1½ lb) ripe honeydew melon,
peeled, seeded and chopped
about 150 ml (¼ pint) water
100 g (4 oz) caster sugar
2 tbls lemon juice
275 ml (10 fl oz) carton double or
whipping cream
25 g (1 oz) piece stem ginger, thinly
sliced
1 tbls ginger syrup*

Purée the melon in a blender. Strain
any juice through a nylon sieve and
make up to 300 ml (½ pint) with water.

Pour the liquid into a heavy-based
saucepan and add the sugar. Heat
gently, stirring, until the sugar has
dissolved. Increase the heat and cook
rapidly until the thread stage is
reached, 107°C (225°F). (To test, remove a little syrup using a small spoon,
and allow it to fall from the spoon on to a

52

dish. The sugar syrup should form a fine thin thread.)

Stir the melon purée and lemon juice into the syrup. Pour the mixture into a rigid freezerproof container and freeze for about 1½ hours until mushy and set around the sides.

Whip the cream until it forms soft peaks. Fold into the frozen melon mixture, with the sliced ginger and ginger syrup. Freeze for a further 3 hours, beating the mixture twice during this time, at hourly intervals.

Nectarine brûlée

SERVES 6

450 g (1 lb) nectarines, stoned and
*   sliced*
350 ml (12 fl oz) soured cream
pinch of grated nutmeg
1 tsp vanilla essence
4 tbls orange liqueur plus extra to
*   flavour fruit*
100 g (4 oz) soft light brown sugar

Cover the nectarines with water in a pan and poach gently for 5-10 minutes or until soft. Drain and transfer to a flameproof casserole. Stir in a little orange-flavoured liqueur.

Beat the soured cream, nutmeg, vanilla and remaining orange liqueur together until blended. Spoon over the nectarine slices then scatter the brown sugar over the top in a thick layer. Grill under a preheated hot grill until the sugar caramelizes.

Serving ideas: Serve with brandy snaps or langue de chat biscuits.
Variations: Use fresh apricots, peaches or pineapple instead of nectarines. Double cream may be used instead of soured cream. The nutmeg may be replaced by cinnamon, and the orange liqueur by rum.

● Left: Melon and ginger ice cream;
Centre: Mango ice cream;
Right: Nectarine brûlée

Passion fruit pavlova

SERVES 8

4 egg whites
225 g (8 oz) caster sugar
1 tsp vanilla essence
1 tsp malt vinegar
2 tsp cornflour
To decorate
450 ml (¾ pint) whipping cream,
  whipped
6 passion fruits

Mark a 23 cm (9 inch) circle on a sheet of non-stick silicone paper or lightly oiled greaseproof paper. Place the paper on a baking sheet. Heat the oven to 150°C, 300°F, Gas Mark 2.

Whisk the egg whites stiffly. Whisk in the sugar a tablespoon at a time until the mixture is thick and glossy, and all the sugar has been used. Fold in the vanilla essence, vinegar and cornflour.

Spoon the mixture inside the marked circle to give a neat round. Using the back of a metal spoon, make a slight well in the centre.

Bake in the oven for 1 hour. Remove from the oven and allow to cool, then transfer carefully to a serving plate.

Spread half the cream over the meringue. Halve the passion fruit and scoop out the pulp with a teaspoon and spoon over the cream. Decorate the pavlova with rosettes or swirls of cream.

Variations: A variety of other fresh fruits may be substituted for the passion fruit. Try a combination of strawberries, pineapple, kiwi fruit, mango and lychees or a mixture of all-red, soft fruits – raspberries, strawberries and redcurrants.

● Left: Persimmon nut loaf;
Centre: Paw paw fluff;
Right: Passion fruit pavlova

Whisk the egg whites until they form soft peaks. Whisk in the sugar, a little at a time, until thick and glossy. Fold into the paw paw mixture. Spoon the mixture into 4 individual glass serving dishes and chill in the refrigerator for at least 2 hours.

Sprinkle the desserts with orange zest and serve.

Persimmon nut loaf

225 g (8 oz) plain flour
1 tsp baking powder
175 g (6 oz) margarine or butter, cut
  into pieces
100 g (4 oz) soft dark brown sugar
225 g (8 oz) fresh persimmons,
  chopped
3 tsp grated orange rind
75 g (3 oz) ground or chopped
  hazelnuts
about 6 tbls soured cream

Grease a 1 kg (2 lb) loaf tin and line the base with greased greaseproof paper. Heat the oven to 180°C, 350°F, Gas Mark 4.

Sift the flour with the baking powder into a bowl. Add the margarine and rub in with the fingertips until the mixture resembles fine breadcrumbs. Stir in the sugar, persimmons, orange rind, hazelnuts and soured cream until combined. Turn the mixture into the prepared loaf tin.

Bake in the oven for 50-60 minutes or until well risen and firm to touch, and a skewer inserted into the centre comes out clean. Turn out on to a wire rack to cool.

Variation: Use walnuts or pecans instead of hazelnuts.

Paw paw fluff

SERVES 4

425 g (15 oz) can paw paw
3 tsp grated orange rind
3 tbls fresh orange juice
15 g (½ oz) sachet powdered gelatine
2 egg whites
50 g (2 oz) caster sugar
shredded orange zest, to decorate

Purée the paw paws with their syrup and the orange rind in a blender.

Put the orange juice in a heatproof bowl, sprinkle over the gelatine and leave for a few minutes until spongy. Put the bowl in a saucepan of hot water and stir until the gelatine has dissolved. Stir into the paw paw purée. Chill in the refrigerator for about 30 minutes until on the point of setting.

Piña colada sorbet

SERVES 4-6

450 ml (¾ pint) pineapple or passion
fruit juice
300 ml (½ pint) water
100 g (4 oz) caster sugar
4 tsp grated lemon rind
3 tbls lemon juice
50 g (2 oz) creamed coconut
2 egg whites

Pour the pineapple juice and water into a heavy-based saucepan and add the sugar, lemon rind and juice. Heat gently, stirring, until the sugar has dissolved. Increase the heat and cook rapidly until the thread stage is reached, 107°C (225°F). (To test, using a small spoon, remove a little syrup and allow it to fall from the spoon on to a dish. The syrup should form a fine thin thread.) Remove from the heat and immediately add the creamed coconut, stirring gently until it melts. Allow to cool.

Pour into a rigid freezerproof container and freeze, stirring occasionally, for about 1½ hours until mushy.

Whisk the egg whites until they form soft peaks. Fold into the pineapple mixture and freeze for a further 3 hours, beating the mixture twice, at hourly intervals.

Sharon fruit fool

SERVES 4

4 sharon fruits, peeled and
chopped
2 tbls caster sugar
3 egg whites
142 ml (5 fl oz) carton double or
whipping cream

Purée the sharon fruit flesh in a blender or food processor. Stir in half the sugar. Chill in the refrigerator for 30 minutes.

Whisk the egg whites stiffly, then whisk in the remaining sugar until glossy.

Whip the cream until it forms soft peaks and fold into the egg whites.

Fold the fruit purée into the cream mixture and spoon into individual glasses. Chill in the refrigerator for at least 2 hours.

Variation: For mango fool, peel a large ripe mango and chop the flesh. Purée, then stir in 25 g (1 oz) caster sugar and 1 tsp lime or lemon juice. Continue as for Sharon fruit fool.

• Sharon fruit fool; Pineapple meringue shortcake; Piña colada sorbet

---

Pineapple meringue shortcake

SERVES 6

250 g (9 oz) plain flour
¼ tsp salt
150 g (5 oz) butter, diced
175 g (6 oz) caster sugar
2 large eggs, separated
1 tbls flaked almonds
a few glacé cherries, to decorate
For the filling
300 g (10 oz) fresh pineapple, chopped
  and drained
142 ml (5 fl oz) carton double cream,
  lightly whipped

Heat the oven to 190°C, 375°F, Gas Mark 5. Sift the flour with the salt into a mixing bowl. Add the butter and rub in with the fingertips until the mixture resembles fine breadcrumbs. Add half the sugar. Beat the egg yolks and add to the dry ingredients. Mix well to form a stiff dough. Turn on to a floured board or work surface and knead the dough lightly until smooth.

Roll out on a greased baking tray to a 23 cm (9 inch) round. Prick all over with a fork. Bake in the oven for 20 minutes, then remove from the oven and reduce the oven temperature to 140°C, 275°F, Gas Mark 1.

Whisk the egg whites until they form stiff peaks. Whisk in the remaining sugar, a teaspoon at a time, until stiff and glossy. Spoon or pipe the meringue round the edge of the shortcake, using a large rose nozzle. Sprinkle with the almonds.

Return to the oven and bake for a further 30 minutes or until the meringue is crisp. Remove from the oven and leave to cool for 10 minutes, then transfer to a wire rack and leave to cool completely.

Fold three-quarters of the pineapple into the cream and spread over the centre of the cake. Decorate with the remaining pineapple and the cherries.

Serving idea: This luxurious cake makes a perfect dinner party dessert.

● Above: Tropical fruit cocktail; Right: Coconut ice and Stuffed dates

Tropical fruit cocktail

SERVES 4

1 ripe paw paw, peeled, seeded and
  diced
1 banana, peeled and chopped
1 small mango, peeled, stoned and
  diced
15 g (½ oz) caster sugar
juice of 1 lime
lime slices, to decorate

Arrange the fruits in layers in a glass
serving dish.

Sprinkle the fruit with the sugar and
lime juice.

Serve well chilled, decorated with
lime slices.

Serving idea: Top each glass with
swirled whipped cream.

Variations: Cantaloup melon or
peaches could be used instead of paw
paw, pineapple instead of mango and
lychees instead of banana and pile the
fruit into a scooped out melon or
pineapple half. Use rum, Cointreau or
Grand Marnier instead of the lime
juice, decorate with an orange slice.

58

Coconut ice

750 g (1½ lb) sugar
300 ml (½ pint) water
2 pinches of cream of tartar
225 g (8 oz) desiccated coconut
a few drops of pink food colouring

Line an 18 cm (7 inch) square tin with greaseproof paper.

Place half the sugar and half the water in a saucepan over a low heat and stir until the sugar has dissolved. Add one pinch of cream of tartar. Bring to the boil and boil to 115°C (238°F), or until a teaspoon of the syrup forms a soft ball when dropped into cold water.

Remove from the heat and stir in half the coconut, all at once. Pour into the prepared tin and chill until set.

Meanwhile, make a second quantity of coconut ice in the same way and stir in a little pink colouring when adding the coconut. Spread over the set layer in the tin and chill in the refrigerator for 1 hour, until set. Cut into squares and wrap each one in waxed paper.

Serving ideas: Coconut ice is ideal as a birthday or Christmas present.

Stuffed dates

MAKES 16

16 fresh dates, halved and stoned
1 tbls kirsch
100 g (4 oz) marzipan
silver balls, halved glacé cherries or
    toasted almonds, to decorate

In a bowl, beat the kirsch into the marzipan. Divide into 16 portions and shape into ovals, to fit into the dates.

Press the marzipan into the dates and gently press the sides of the dates together slightly over the marzipan. Decorate with silver balls or pieces of glacé cherry and place in petits fours cases, if liked. Leave to set in a cool place for at least 1 hour.

Serving ideas: Serve with after-dinner coffee or make as a gift at Christmas time.
Variations: The marzipan-filled dates may be dipped in melted plain chocolate to coat, then decorated with glacé cherries.

The dates may be filled with shelled Brazil nuts instead of marzipan.

Pineapple with chocolate fondue

SERVES 4

225 g (8 oz) plain chocolate, broken
  into pieces
142 ml (5 fl oz) carton double cream
100 g (4 oz) marshmallows
1 pineapple, peeled, cored and cut
  into 2.5 cm (1 inch) cubes

Place the chocolate and the cream in a
fondue pot or heatproof bowl set over a
saucepan of simmering water over a
gentle heat. Stir for about 5 minutes
until the chocolate has melted. Add the
marshmallows and stir for a further 5
minutes until melted. Do not allow the
fondue to boil and keep over a low heat.

Arrange the pineapple on a serving
dish. To serve, spear the pineapple with
fondue forks and dip into the chocolate
fondue.

Serving ideas: Serve as a sweetmeat or
dessert.

Variations: Add 50 g (2 oz) toasted
chopped almonds to the fondue.

Use other fruits, such as strawberries or banana slices coated in lemon
juice, to dip into the fondue.

Banana yoghurt shake

SERVES 2-4

600 ml (1 pint) milk, chilled
2 large ripe bananas, peeled
300 ml (½ pint) hazelnut yoghurt,
  chilled
2 tbls caster sugar

Place all the ingredients in a blender
and process for 10-15 seconds until
smooth. Pour into tall glasses and serve
immediately.

Serving ideas: Decorate the yoghurt
shake with banana slices dipped in
lemon juice to prevent discoloration
and chopped roasted hazelnuts: serve
as a dessert rather than a drink, with
long-handled spoons.

Variations: Use mandarin, strawberry
or lemon flavoured yoghurt instead of
hazelnut yoghurt.

Use 12 canned apricot halves,
drained, or 6 peeled fresh ripe apricots,
instead of the banana. 4-6 pineapple
rings, roughly chopped, or ripe strawberries, may also be substituted for the
banana.

● Left to right: Pineapple with chocolate
fondue; Apricot-pineapple frost; Banana
yoghurt shake; Grapefruit and orange
cooler

Grapefruit and orange cooler

SERVES 1

1 sugar lump
1 orange
2 measures (45 ml/1 1/2 fl oz) orange juice
2 measures (45 ml/1 1/2 fl oz) grapefruit juice
crushed ice or ice cubes
soda water
orange slice, to decorate

Rub the sugar lump over the orange rind to release the oil. Place in a tumbler.

Stir the orange and grapefruit juices together with ice. Strain into the tumbler and top up with soda water. Add crushed ice, decorate with the orange slice and serve with a straw and cocktail umbrella.

Variation: Pineapple juice may be used instead of grapefruit.

Apricot-pineapple frost

SERVES 4

425 g (15 oz) can apricots
150 ml (1/4 pint) unsweetened pineapple juice
1/2 tsp peppermint essence
crushed ice
4 mint sprigs, to decorate

Place the apricots with their syrup, the pineapple juice and peppermint essence in a blender and process until puréed and frothy.

Pour over crushed ice in 4 tall glasses and decorate each one with a mint sprig. Serve immediately.

Variation: Canned peaches may replace the apricots.

Sunrise cocktail

SERVES 1

1 measure (45 ml/1½ fl oz) orange
*   juice*
1 measure (45 ml/1½ fl oz) dry
*   vermouth*
dash of orange bitters
crushed ice
. 2 lemon slices or 1 orange slice,
*   to decorate*

Shake the orange juice, vermouth and
orange bitters together with ice in a
cocktail shaker. Strain into a chilled
cocktail glass. Place 2 lemon slices on
the rim of the glass to decorate.

After-dinner cocktail

SERVES 1

1 measure (45 ml/1½ fl oz) apricot
*   brandy*
½ measure (20 ml/¾ fl oz) Cointreau
1 tbls fresh lime juice
crushed ice
lime slices, to decorate

Shake the brandy, Cointreau and lime
juice together with ice in a cocktail
shaker. Strain into a chilled cocktail
glass. Decorate the glass with the lime
slices.

● Left to right: Knockout cocktail,
After-dinner cocktail, Bacardi special,
Sunrise cocktail, Far East cocktail

Knockout cocktail

SERVES 1

1 measure (45 ml/1½ fl oz) dry
*   vermouth*
1 measure (45 ml/1½ fl oz) whisky
1 measure (45 ml/1½ fl oz) pineapple
*   juice*
crushed ice
piece of pineapple, to decorate

Shake the vermouth, whisky and
pineapple juice together with ice in a
cocktail shaker. Strain into a chilled
cocktail glass and decorate with the
piece of pineapple.

Variation: Sweet vermouth may be
used instead of dry.

Far East cocktail

SERVES 1

1 measure (45 ml/1½ fl oz) orange
Curaçao
1 measure (45 ml/1½ fl oz) brandy
1 measure (45 ml/1½ fl oz) pineapple
juice
dash of Angostura bitters
crushed ice
To decorate
piece of pineapple
orange slice
1 cocktail cherry

Shake the Curaçao, brandy, pineapple juice and bitters together with crushed ice in a cocktail shaker. Strain into a chilled cocktail glass. Spear the fruit on to a cocktail stick and use to decorate the glass.

Bacardi special

SERVES 1

1 measure (45 ml/1½ fl oz) gin
2 measures (90 ml/3 fl oz) Bacardi rum
1 tsp grenadine
2 tsp fresh lime juice
crushed ice
strip of thinly pared lime rind, to
decorate

Shake the gin, rum, grenadine and lime juice together with ice in a cocktail shaker. Strain into a chilled cocktail glass and place the lime rind on the rim.

Variation: Omit the gin and increase the grenadine and fresh lime juice to 1 tbls each.

INDEX

Note: this index includes variations suggested in recipes as well as the main recipes. Lists of vegetables and fruits on pp.5-15 have not been included in index as they are already in alphabetical order.